for Trish
Blessings
Carole Harris Barton

When God Gets Physical

**True Stories of People Who Heard
God's Voice, Felt His Touch
or Saw a Sign of
His Presence**

Carole Harris Barton

Lakewood Ranch, Florida

WHEN GOD GETS PHYSICAL
by Carole Harris Barton

Published by Outcome Publishing
11523 Palm Brush Trail #372
Lakewood Ranch, Florida 34202
www.outcomepublishing.com

This book or parts thereof may not be reproduced in any form, stored in a retrieval system, or transmitted in any form by any means – electronic, mechanical, photocopy, recording, or otherwise – without prior written permission of the publisher, except as provided by United States of America copyright law.

All scripture quotations, unless otherwise indicated, are taken from the Holy Bible, New International Version.® NIV®. Copyright ©1973, 1978, 1984 by International Bible Society. Used by permission of Zondervan. All rights reserved.

Copyright © 2009 by Carole Harris Barton
All rights reserved

Edited by Teri Hayden

Cover Design by Leeann Martin

First Edition

Printed in the United States of America

1. Religion: Spirituality General
2. Self-Help: Spiritual
3. Religion: Christian Life – Personal Growth

What People Are Saying About
When God Gets Physical

A series of vignettes that individually may be described as ethereal or enigmatic, or perhaps both. Magnificently written and truly inspirational, they collectively represent a must-read for all who long for a glimpse of glory. – Marvin G. Gregory, M.D., J.D., Nashville, Tennessee

These stories are like potato chips. You can't read just one. – Anonymous

Spiritually written with a sweet grace that presents living examples of an unseen dimension of love, nurturing, and sometimes warning. Essential for anyone seeking to resonate with the creative Being who uses multiple media to address us personally. – James F. Hoffman, Jr., Th.D., Pastor, Minister, and Spiritual Director, Fairfax, Virginia

~~~

also by
Carole Harris Barton
Rainbows in Coal Country

*for the people who trusted me to
tell their stories and made this
book theirs as much as mine*

Contents

Acknowledgements

Writing this book was like going on a journey without a map. Only with the help of many people did I reach my destination. I am indebted to those who shared their experiences for publication, of course, but also those who supported my journey in progress. The women of Skycrest United Methodist Church in Clearwater, Florida, believed in my work from the moment they heard about it and gave me more encouragement than they know. My husband, Paul, reminded me to eat by plying me with food from our kitchen when I spent long hours at my computer, not once threatening to dump me in favor of someone who would make a hot meal for him every evening. My brother and his wife, John and Gretchen Harris, and my stepson and his wife, Mark and Lynne Barton, read my first draft and made insightful suggestions that greatly improved it. Dr. Marvin Gregory helped me with the reporting of medical facts and encouraged me to believe my manuscript was worthy of publication. Vivian West breathed life into the waning embers of my endurance with her unflagging support. Nancy Studebaker held my hands in hers and prayed that God would lead me to a publisher, and he led me to Mary Courtney, who introduced me to Outcome Publishing. The entire staff of this dedicated Christian firm embraced my work and offered me their unfailing professionalism and personal courtesy. Thank you, my family, friends, and colleagues.

Introduction

God is spirit, but sometimes he gets physical. I know this because, like many biblical characters, I have experienced the presence of God through my physical senses: once through a dream that relieved my grief after my father died and once through a healing that instantly stopped my bleeding and saved the life of my unborn baby.

So astounding and so holy were these experiences that I told no one, but I didn't forget. How common was such an experience? How uncommon? And if everyone who had such an experience treated it as confidentially as I had, how would I ever find out? But if I could find out, a collection of such accounts would make a God-honoring inspirational book, wouldn't it? The person and the problem + the physical presence of God = positive change. What a theme!

In 2002, I began to query my friends and acquaintances at church and community groups. "I'm writing a book," I would say. "Have you ever experienced the presence of God through something you saw, heard, or felt in a physical sense?" Through an informal system of referrals the stories began to trickle in, and based on interviews and correspondence, I began to write. When I had about 25,000 words—less than half that needed for an average-sized book—I reached a logjam. With no new stories coming my way, I shelved the manuscript of my "God book" and wrote my memoir, *Rainbows in Coal Country*, published in 2005. Still, my God book was on the back burner. I hadn't forgotten it, but how could I write a book of true stories when a logjam was blocking my access to true stories?

One Sunday in the spring of 2008, I mulled over my dilemma as I drove home from church. It was almost time to leave my winter home in Florida and return to Virginia for the summer, and I still had no idea what to do about my manuscript. Perhaps I didn't have the beginnings of a book after all; perhaps I had some magazine articles or e-zine pieces.

It was time for a go/no-go decision. "God," I said as I parked my car in front of my condo, "if you want me to write this book, send me the stories so I'll know. And if you do, I promise to write them." I got out of my car, walked about halfway up the path to my front door, and there on the walk lay a brownish-beige feather about eight inches long. Unaware of the adage that a person who finds a feather is on an ascending spiritual journey, I picked the feather up and put it in my journal for a bookmark.

A few days later in Virginia, I opened an email containing a referral to someone with a story for my book. I went for the interview and met a woman who told me about finding a feather and the significant spiritual experience that followed. *What a story,* I thought as I drove home with notes for "Feather." I got out of my car, walked about halfway up the path to my front door, and there on the walk lay a yellowish-beige feather about two inches long.

What? Another feather? Suddenly, like a jigsaw puzzle, the separate pieces of my experience began to fall into place: a feather, a story about a feather, and another feather within 10 days in two different states a thousand miles apart, and never before had I found a feather. I picked it up and saved it because—Knock me on the head with a feather!—surely it was heavenly acknowledgement of my feather story.

But it was more than that. The next day I received a referral to another story, and the day after that to another, and then another and another. If two feathers can break a logjam, these had, and new stories began to come my way so fast that I couldn't finish one before another story appeared. I continued to follow the trail of my referrals and 35,000 words later, this book is the result.

Is that a God story or just a collection of feathers?

Whatever you may think, the timing was perfect, because when I started to work again, I discovered that during my fallow years, the National Opinion Research Center of the University of Chicago had released a report[1] that answered some of my questions. Half of Americans say they have had at least one religious or spiritual experience that transformed their life for the better; for about 17 percent of the half, the experience was physical. They saw an angel or a bright light, heard God's audible voice, felt either an out-of-body or a floating sensation, received a supernatural healing, had a dream or a waking vision, felt enveloped in a blanket of warmth, established contact with the dead, saw an event of nature (a rainbow, snowstorm, or lightening, for example) at just the right time, or received another physical sign. Yet few gave a description of the event.

Just the information I needed: Other people had reported spiritual or religious experiences similar to mine but had not described them. What other reason did I need to write a book describing such experiences?

One of two types of events usually preceded these experiences, said the report. People were involved in religious activity or they were facing some type of personal problem or big life change—they fought illness, lost their job, crashed their car, or watched a loved one die. In the process, they experienced the presence of God.

One of the most widely reported twentieth century experiences happened to the late Martin Luther King, Jr., early in his struggle for civil rights. Frightened and sleepless after anonymous phone calls threatened him with death, King went to the kitchen in the middle of the night, made a pot of coffee, sat down at the table, and confessed to God that he was worried. Then came an audible voice. "Martin Luther, stand up for righteousness. Stand up for justice. Stand up for truth...."[2] King experienced the presence of God, he said. Almost at once, his fear left him and he went on to lead the march for civil rights in the United States.

But not everybody who encounters a personal supernatural power is religious. Bill Sinkford, president of the Unitarian Universalist Association in 2008, went from being a self-described "stand-up atheist" to a believer in God when his adolescent son was hospitalized for a drug overdose. "While sitting beside his bed in the hospital...I had an experience of being held," said Sinkford. "I knew that I was being held and supported, and somehow I knew that my son was, as well...I found that presence incredibly hopeful...I came to develop a prayer life, and I no longer consider myself an atheist."[3]

This book presents 37 true stories of people who experienced the presence of God through one or more of their physical senses. True to the pattern noted in the National Opinion Research Center survey, some of the people I interviewed reported having more than one experience, and in some cases, God personally appeared. The witness heard his voice, felt his touch, or saw the face or form of Jesus—God personified—in a dream or waking vision. In other cases, a sign appeared that denoted God's presence; for example, a star streaked across the sky just after a woman asked God for a sign that he had heard her prayer, and she recognized the shooting star as God using his created order to send a message of support.

The key to both types of experiences is that the individual's physical senses were tools of observation and the spiritual sense was a tool of interpretation.

These stories, more than the typical "I was in trouble and God helped" variety, take the reader through the experience with the person by setting the event within the context of the character and life circumstance of the witness—for only in the human context does the event have meaning.

These experiences are similar to those of many biblical characters who encountered God in a more dramatic and physical way than might be expected of the invisible and silent God who is present everywhere and all the time. For example, God appeared to Solomon in a dream. Solomon heard God's voice, talked with him, and received a gift of wisdom to lead his people (I Kings 3:4-12). In another case, when two pregnant women got together for a visit, Elizabeth felt her unborn baby move and instantly knew that her cousin Mary was carrying the Son of God (Luke 1:39-45).

Like those biblical people, the contemporary people whose stories I tell—all of whom seem to accept that God, Jesus, and the Holy Spirit are aspects of the same being— did not explain how they knew that God was the origin of the event and did not explain how they knew what it meant. They just knew. Job, arguably the oldest book in the Bible, affirms the reality and value of spiritual knowledge when Elihu comforts Job and silences his critics: "It is the spirit in a man, the breath of the Almighty, that gives him understanding" (Job 32:8, NIV).

The events in this book, with a few notable exceptions, occurred when the witness was alone. Does that cast doubt on the validity of the experiences? Not if measured by the standard of similar biblical accounts in which the witness was alone.

Could these events be nothing more than coincidence, especially those in which a natural or environmental event is understood to be a symbol of God's presence? Yes, assuming coincidence exists. Some people accept the concept while rejecting the reality; they believe God uses seemingly random unexplained events to accomplish his overall purpose.

Could the contributors have fabricated their stories? Admittedly, my approach was to listen and report, not to challenge and prove. If this gives you pause, do as I did. Strike the stories against the bell of your reality and listen for the ring of truth. Perhaps one contributor spoke for all when he said, "I don't care whether people believe me or not. God was speaking to me, not them. But if my story helps someone else, that's good."

The contributors represent no particular religious affiliation and espouse no specific theology or set of beliefs. Their ages at the time of the experience range from a nine-year-old boy to a woman in her seventies; their geographic locations range from Florida to California and from the United States to Africa. With a few exceptions, each account identifies the contributor. When people requested anonymity, I disguised their identity and used fictitious names and locations in the account. Of 37 stories, including two of my own, only four are anonymous.

In doing this work, I sometimes felt I was standing on holy ground. Often I struggled to maintain my composure as my interviewees, many of whom had never before described the experience, shed tears or their voices choked and words faltered. At other times, I marveled at how unemotionally a moving story unfolded. But always, real people spoke of encountering a real God in a real world. I feel immensely complimented that friends and strangers alike opened their hearts and showed me their treasures. I value their trust and I honor it by telling their stories as faithfully as I can.

Why does God sometimes reveal himself in ways people can see, hear, or touch, and other times make his presence known through a gentle whisper (I Kings 19:12, NIV) that some biblical translations call a "still small voice"? The answer is his. To me, the mystery of God's presence is just that: a mystery.

"I will tell of the kindnesses of the Lord, the deeds for which he is to be praised...." reads Isaiah 63:7, NIV. As Isaiah spoke to the people, so I speak to you. And the stories speak for themselves.

Table

The man who thinks he knows something
does not yet know as he ought to know.
I Corinthians 8:2

O nce, for about five minutes just after he passed the test for his driver's license, he might have thought he knew it all—or at least, everything that mattered. But that was when he was a teenager.

John was beyond that now, and on this Sunday morning prior to administering communion, he was delivering a sermon on the Eucharist. Nearing his fiftieth year of ordination, he took the occasion to share an experience of administering communion as a young graduate student at the seminary.

It was 1964 and he had four years experience as a pastor—enough that he had learned, even with an undergraduate degree and a divinity degree from the seminary, he didn't know it all. So back he went to Southern Baptist Theological Seminary in Louisville, Kentucky, to enroll in a Master's program majoring in pastoral care. Now he would learn what really mattered. Through a process of study, practice, and reflection, always under the supervision of qualified professors, he would receive clinical training in ministering to people in situations of crisis or illness.

A specified number of hours in a clinical setting was a requirement for the degree, and the seminary assigned John to work in the chaplaincy program at Central State Hospital. An adult psychiatric residential hospital, it is sited in a secluded rural setting in eastern Jefferson County just outside Louisville.

1

Some hospital residents, known at the time as patients, had mental illnesses and some had mental retardation. Some patients were ambulatory without assistance; others had physical disabilities requiring them to use wheelchairs or other devices to aid their mobility. Some patients had lived there from a few weeks to a few months; others had been resident for years and would spend the rest of their lives there. Some patients had family members or friends who visited from time to time, and some never had outside visitors except for the clergy. For the latter patients, their only other human interaction coming from staff or other patients, visits from the clergy took on great importance.

One day, John's supervising chaplain asked him to remain after hours to conduct a worship service and administer communion.

Call it the Eucharist, the Lord's Supper, or the Last Supper. Define it as a rite, a sacrament, or a remembrance. Serve grape juice and cubes of yeast bread or serve wine and pinches of unleavened bread. Serve it only in a designated house of worship or serve it in homes, hospitals, prisons, or anywhere worshipers are unable to attend church. Allow only ordained clergy to administer it or authorize lay Christians to administer it.

With almost as many ways of observing communion as there are Christian denominations, about the only thing universally agreed upon is that ever since Jesus ate the bread and drank the cup with his disciples, Christians have observed communion. "Do this in remembrance of me," Jesus said (Luke 22:19, NIV). So Christians do—a practice that has endured for centuries. Regardless of the differing beliefs about communion and the differing modes of administering it, the elements represent the body and blood of Jesus Christ.

Table

2

John prepared the elements. Given the varying religious backgrounds of the patients, the service would be nondenominational in nature. And given the differing mental states and physical abilities of the patients, the only way safely to administer the elements was for John to dip a wafer into a cup of wine and place the wafer on the tongue of the open-mouthed recipient.

Suzy, a woman in her 60s, sat in a chair against a wall away from other people. Resident at Central State for many years, she had been catatonic and entirely mute for the last ten of them.

John read a scripture and presented a short devotional. Afterward, as he stood leading the 20-30 worshipers in singing a hymn, he noticed Suzy moving her lips. It was not typical of her, but he was too far away to hear whether she was emitting sound. After the hymn, John began the service of communion, working his way around the room. When he reached Suzy, he dipped a wafer into the cup and placed the wine-soaked wafer on her tongue. In a routine manner, Suzy swallowed it. Then, in a non-routine manner, she spoke. "Thank you, sir," she said, quite lucidly and quite clearly—her first words in a decade.

"God bless you," said an astonished John.

The next morning, the event was the topic of discussion at the professional staff meeting. A religious experience discussed at a medical staff meeting? Yes, something almost as rare as was the event that led to the discussion. Never before had the staff seen anything like what happened, and only rarely had they read of anything similar in medical literature or heard of it in clinical practice. A catatonic person, mute for years, had spoken.

Table

3

If seasoned professionals had no explanation for what happened, neither did John. Except that at the table of the Lord, something happened—something wonderfully mysterious and moving. Was Jesus the Christ in the elements of the bread and the wine? Yes, either in symbolic form or in reality.

John didn't know it all in the 1960s when he returned to the seminary for additional education, he didn't know it all when Suzy spoke that day in the hospital, and he didn't know it all in 2008 when he shared the experience with his church members before serving communion.

But he knew more after Suzy spoke than he knew before. He knew that when Christians come to the table of the Lord, they ought to come expecting something wonderfully mysterious to happen. And when they leave, they ought to say, "Thank you, Sir."

- -

Since this event in the hospital, John M. Harris has shared the experience with every church he has served, including churches in Kentucky, South Carolina, and Florida. At this writing, he is Interim Pastor of Hope Presbyterian Church in Largo, Florida.

Table

4

Play

On my bed I remember you; I think of you through
the watches of the night. Because you are my help, I
sing in the shadow of your wings.
Psalm 63:6-7

Except for his washed out jeans instead of rolled up
pantaloons, he could have been the poet's barefoot boy
whistling tunes in the sunshine. And except that it was the
1950s instead of the 1850s.

He was nine years old, a towheaded lad with eyes as
blue as the skies and enough curiosity to kill the proverbial
cat. It was mid-May and nobody had told Tommy that
summer wouldn't start until June 21. Nobody had told
summer, either. Summer showed it by raising the heat early
in the day. Tommy showed it by abandoning his shoes to
the underside of his bed.

In Columbus, Georgia, just a few miles from the
Chattahoochee River, Tommy's world was much the same
as the 1850s New England world of poet John Greenleaf
Whittier's barefoot boy. Squirrels and frogs; hummingbirds
and fireflies. Black wasps and their walls of clay; black
spiders and their webs of silk. Minnows in a sand-rimmed
millpond and boyhood's painless play. And the pure joy of
bare feet.

Ah, the comfort of toes unencumbered by shoes! Ouch,
the discomfort of tender feet not yet tough enough to
tolerate the occasional sharp pebble or broken twig, or the
blistering heat of the sun-baked earth. The foot-toughening
process would happen gradually over the summer, but until
then, a barefoot boy had to watch the ground beneath his
feet like a hawk watches its prey. Otherwise, a minor injury

5

could force him to sit out the pretend sword fights in which boys brandished the ubiquitous foot-long seedpods of the catalpa tree to conquer imaginary pirates of the high seas, or relegate him to the sidelines of a raucous game of hide-and-seek.

Tommy loved summer, especially the part about not going to school. He was very smart and didn't object to school all that much, but he didn't love it, either. At school, boys had to study stuff and girls got to do stuff—mainly, show off the stuff they already knew, it seemed to Tommy. Girls! He tolerated them the way he tolerated school. He had enough energy for two little boys and he would much rather do stuff than study stuff.

Today Tommy had lots of stuff to do. It was Wednesday morning and construction workers had already arrived to build a back porch onto his family's house. It predated by years the arrival of electric household appliances, and without the back porch, the Watleys would have no place to locate their must-have refrigerator, freezer chest, and wringer washing machine, to say nothing of the collectibles the family never used but never trashed.

Tommy didn't know exactly what his family intended for their new back porch, but he knew what he intended. He intended to see it built. What he didn't know was that he was about to put to rest Whittier's myth of boyhood's painless play.

Tommy snooped in the men's toolboxes, examined the heaps of roofing shingles stashed on the ground, and poked around the stacks of new lumber. How did the men know what to do, Tommy wondered. When he grew up maybe he would be a carpenter and build houses. He liked saws and hammers, the sturdy multi-pocketed work aprons the men wore to keep their tools handy, and the trucks they drove to carry their supplies. Tommy was careful to stay out of the way; otherwise, he was apt to get his rear end swatted. He knew that danger. He did not know the danger of an active construction site.

Tommy was checking out a pile of debris where the men had ripped out the back doorsteps to make way for the porch when a sharp pain suddenly stabbed him in the foot. Yow-eee—a nail! Embedded in a 1x4-inch board tossed aside by one of the workers, the up-ended nail had punctured Tommy's foot, completely burying itself in his left heel and literally nailing the barefoot boy to the board.

Tommy screamed. The men turned in unison and ran to the immobilized boy, his face contorted in pain and his cheeks scalded with tears. "Lay him down, lay him down," someone urged excitedly. And Tommy's father forcibly held his screaming son to the ground as one of the other men grabbed both ends of the board and yanked. With one swift motion, board and 16-penny nail came loose, the nail's sharp point and three inches of rusty steel dripping Tommy's blood.

Raw, searing, saw-toothed pain slashed a swath of agony all the way from Tommy's foot to his knee as he lay writhing on the ground.

The Watleys were members of the Fifteenth Street Church of God. They believed in the verbal inspiration of the Bible, water baptism by immersion of all who repent of their sins, washing the feet of the saints, and speaking in other tongues as the Spirit gives utterance. And they believed in divine healing as provided in the atonement of Jesus. The Watleys did not seek medical help.

The small group of family and workers gathered around Tommy praying and pleading aloud for God's help as Tommy's mother, who had run out of the house when she heard the commotion, gathered some rags. Hurriedly she wet a rag with kerosene poured from a nearby can, tore strips from another rag to make ties, and wrapped Tommy's foot in a makeshift bandage. As the praying continued, the boy's shrieks gradually dwindled into soft whimpers and finally stopped. He had begun to absorb the shock of the accident, and with the comfort of so many caring adults, he could handle it.

Hours later, hobbling around inside the house on tiptoe, Tommy could not lower his heel to the floor. Throughout the day, his mother repeatedly removed the bloody bandage and applied a clean one, making a final change at bedtime.

A night of pain is a long night. Tommy could not sleep, his foot pulsating in a driving pain that forced him into an involuntary cycle of tossing and turning as he searched in vain for a hint of relief. The next morning, the pain was so intense that the mere effort of trying to touch his foot to the floor increased the strength of the throbbing.

Tommy stayed in bed. Would his foot burst? He felt as if it might, and the pounding pressure felt less severe when his foot was elevated. His mother periodically brought him food and water, but he ate little and drank only the few swallows he could force down. Occasionally he arose to limp to the bathroom, but having consumed so little food and drink, his trips were infrequent.

Tetanus, the infectious disease people often associate with a wound from a rusty nail, was not a concern because Tommy had been inoculated as a requirement for enrollment in public school. But wound contamination by other bacteria was a real possibility, and something was causing Tommy's pain to continue, even if not the dreadful disease commonly known as lockjaw.

Thursday, Friday, Saturday. The swelling expanded. The redness spread. The fluid oozed. The clock ticked. Saturday night, Tommy put off his boyhood and put on his manhood. Saturday night, Tommy took charge.

Church had always been a part of Tommy's life. He was comfortable there and he loved the music that was an important part of worship in the Church of God. Early on, his parents had discovered their son's natural gift for music. Once he heard a song, he could repeat it easily—and he did—no urging, no begging, and no bribing. When he was five years old, his mother dressed him in a freshly ironed shirt, combed his hair, and stood him in front of the adults at church. "I saw the light, I saw the light, praise the Lord, I saw the light,"[4] sang the smiling preschooler—his pitch perfect, his tone pure, his diction clear. The people loved it, and Tommy loved that they loved it. Later, he would see this as a foreshadowing of his future, but at the time, it was just something he liked to do.

But singing wasn't the only thing Tommy had learned at church. He also had learned that offering a prayer in faith can make a sick person well (James 5:15). Tommy was certain that he qualified as a sick person. For four days, he had left the praying to the adults; now he took responsibility for himself. Unreservedly and with all his barefoot-boy heart, he believed that God could heal him. Lying in bed in the dark, he began to pray—earnestly, pleadingly, and with faith—begging for God's help.

Oh! What's that? Someone was in the room with Tommy! In the dim light of night, he widened his eyes and peered through the blackness. No, his mother had not come to change his bandage. No, his father had not come to check on him. Tommy's eyes swept the room. Nothing. Then a gentle touch, like the tickly prance of a butterfly dancing, moved across his heel. "Tomorrow you will be okay," said a voice, sweet and light. "You will be able to walk."

Tommy slept.

The next morning, he remembered it all—the touch, the voice, everything. He had fully expected help, but he had not expected God to make a personal appearance. Still, Tommy was just a boy. What did he know? If this was God's way, it was all right with Tommy.

Gingerly, Tommy touched his wounded foot to the floor. No pain. He stood up and transferred all of his 75 pounds onto his wounded foot. No pain. He sat down and removed the bandage. The swelling was gone, the redness vanished! *Thank you, God.*

Tommy knew about boys in the Bible who had encountered the Almighty. The shepherd boy David spent many nights in the hills with only his sheep, his poetry, and God for company. A boy named Joseph wore a coat of many colors, and when his jealous brothers tried to kill him, he forgave them. An unnamed boy brought a lunch of five loaves and two fishes to Jesus and helped him feed at least 5,000 people.

But Tommy wasn't like those boys, writing poems, wearing princely robes, and doing things so important that people recorded them in the Bible. Tommy was just a barefoot boy in the flatlands of Georgia who went out to play and stepped on a nail. Just a barefoot boy who lay on his bed through the watches of night and remembered God. Just a barefoot boy.

> Blessings on thee, little man,
> Barefoot boy with cheek of tan.[5]

- -

Thomas P. Watley, President of Watley Heating and Air Conditioning, Inc., Columbus, Georgia, is owner and lead singer of The Proclaimers Quartet, www.tpq4him.com. Because God was—and is—Tommy's help, he stands in the shadow of God's wings and sings the praises of God all over the South and the mid-Atlantic states. Another of Tommy's experiences is told in "Song."

Tamarisk

*Abraham planted a tamarisk tree in Beersheba, and
there he called upon the name of the Lord, the
Eternal God.
Genesis 21:33*

Abraham had his tamarisk tree and Rachel had hers.
Abraham's tree was in the desert of the Middle East
centuries ago. Rachel's tree was in the mountains of
Kentucky in the 1980s. Abraham's tree was one of many
thought to have provided the manna that sustained the
Israelites during their wanderings (Exodus 16:31). Rachel's
tree was one of many known to have provided cooling
shade for the Hayes family during their hardscrabble
struggles.

Except that Rachel's tree was a mature maple, not a
young tamarisk.

It didn't matter. Rachel was an informal Bible student
and she knew that the tamarisk, sometimes called the "tree
of life" because a small sap-sucking insect turns the sap
into a sweet honey-like substance that drops to the ground
to be harvested and eaten, had a twofold purpose. It was
meant to bless the stomach, yes—but it also was meant to
bless the spirit of the people who used it as a reminder to
call on the name of the Lord.

Anyone who saw Rachel under the tree and knew what
was going on inside the nearby log cabin might have
thought she had gone to the tree to escape. She hadn't. She
had gone to her tamarisk to call on the name of the Lord—
not to ask God to heal her mother, but to ask him to prevent

her suffering. A widow now 84, Goldie had been ill almost three months. Like many an ill person, her appetite had wasted away and so had she. She had not eaten for days. It all started with what Goldie called stomach trouble. When it became chronic, her doctor performed surgery for what he thought was probably gall bladder disease. It wasn't; it was cirrhosis of the liver, likely the aftermath of a bout with hepatitis years earlier.

Goldie survived the surgery but afterward lapsed into a light coma. Many an hour Rachel sat beside her mother's bedside praying incessantly and drawing solace from the cross-topped church spire that reached for the sky outside the hospital window. The spire wasn't as good as Rachel's tamarisk, but it would do. Finally, Goldie pulled out of the coma. *Thank you, God,* thought Rachel, hugging her mother and returning home.

Five days later, her siblings called Rachel back to their mother's bedside. This time, Goldie's kidneys were failing. She pulled through but she was very weak and her doctor transferred her to a nursing home. She hated it with a passion and was ecstatic a few days later when doctors released her. "Glory, hallelujah, I'm going home," she rejoiced when Rachel rolled her outside in a wheelchair. "Going home" meant going home to hospice care.

Home was Ed Hayes' log cabin in Candy Holler where Goldie had moved as the railroad worker's young bride in the 1930s. Set in the verdant foothills of the Kentucky mountains, Candy Holler was a hill country mispronunciation of Canada Hollow. The term, a throwback to the Prohibition era, denoted a secluded valley that hid the stills where mountaineers brewed corn whisky as good as any sold legally in Canada.

Sited at the end of a dirt road with a mountain at its back, the log cabin Ed had built with his own hands from trees he had personally hewn could be approached only from the front. With the grit of a true mountain woman, Goldie had unflinchingly stepped into her role as stepmother to Ed's three little girls left behind when his first wife had abandoned Ed. Rachel was the first of six more children later born into the family.

It was a hard life but the family knew no one with an easier one. The nation was recovering from the Great Depression, and people were grateful for every morsel of food and every scrap of clothing they could collect. The family had plenty to wear, Goldie said—"Wash one and wear one." And they had plenty of food: vegetables from their garden; meat, eggs, and milk from their farm animals. Progress came slowly, but Ed later enlarged the log cabin, eventually adding a hand pump to bring water to the kitchen from the outside well, and then adding wiring for electric lights and a few kitchen appliances.

Now far removed from Candy Holler and living in a modern house, Rachel was happily married and a mother. Well served by an education begun in a rural schoolhouse, she was a health professional adept at engaging with medical personnel and competent to negotiate the complexities of the health care system. She was the best choice of all the offspring to cope with Goldie's illness, so she took a leave of absence from her job to return to the log cabin. There Rachel had retreated to the front yard and her tamarisk to pray when Bea, Goldie's home health caregiver, shouted for help.

Rachel rushed inside to find the bodice of her mother's gown damp and freshly soiled. "Who was that doctor who was just here?" Goldie asked. "He said if I could upchuck, I would be hungry again. He was the nicest man, and he was very handsome."

"No, Mom, no one is here but Bea and me," said Rachel as Bea brought towels and a basin of warm soapy water.

Goldie may have been ill, but she still had the presence of mind to distinguish between past and present tense, and she had the spunk to be annoyed when not taken seriously. "I know. I didn't say he *is* here," she protested as Rachel and Bea bathed her and changed her into a clean gown. "I said he *was* here."

Rachel and Bea looked knowingly at each other. It was not unusual for a gravely ill person to hallucinate. "No, Mom," Rachel repeated. "I have been outside in the front yard the whole time and Bea has been inside with you. If the doctor had been here, we would have seen him. No one has been here today but us."

"Don't argue with me, child," ordered an unconvinced Goldie. Then, entirely lucid and aware of a hunger she had not felt for days, she sent Rachel off to make dinner.

Alone in the kitchen, a glimmer of insight filtered through Rachel's initial bewilderment, then gradually expanded to full comprehension. For days, she had gone to her tamarisk and begged God for his mercy, but had unconsciously placed limits on how that mercy might be delivered. Rachel now mentally removed those limits. Like cumulus clouds drifting across blue sky, her burden drifted away as she saw the truth.

Goldie ate her dinner that night, and in the days that followed, she continued not just to eat, but to enjoy her food and the visitors who came to her bedside. Not a single moment did she suffer during the next three weeks before dying peacefully in her sleep, and she never knew what happened the day her appetite returned.

But Rachel knew. She knew that day in the kitchen, the very day she looked out the window at her tamarisk and thanked God for filling her mother's stomach with food as nourishing as manna from heaven. And for sending the angel.

- -

Rachel Hayes Wade, a watercolorist and mammographer in Lynchburg, Virginia, whose work helped save many women from breast cancer, lost her own battle to that disease in 2005. One of her favorite paintings was the view from the log cabin described in this story.

Breath

*Then Judas (not Judas Iscariot) said, "But, Lord,
why do you intend to show yourself to us and not to
the world?" Jesus replied, "If anyone loves me, he
will obey my teaching. My Father will love him, and
we will come to him and make our home with him."*
John 14:22-23

It had been a long day. But not just a long day, also a
bad day. Not 9/11 bad, just regular bad. Like when Alice
forgot to return the milk to the refrigerator after breakfast,
and the cat scratched her when she put it in the carrier to go
to the vet, and a tire on her car went flat, and it rained and
she didn't have her umbrella. That kind of bad day.

Alice drove home from the office, stopped her car and
got out. She walked to the front door, let herself in, and
switched on the light. Trudging wearily down the hallway,
she quietly entered her bedroom. There in the privacy of
her own space, she gave herself permission to admit what
she had not yet dared to think. After months of preparation,
things still were not working out.

Alice was usually a positive person; it was part of how
she defined her Christian faith. But she was also an
emotionally honest person. And to be honest with herself,
she had to acknowledge that this had been the worst day
since the project began, absolutely the worst.

It was Alice's job to bring technological change to the
university classroom. Every lecture, every handout, every
visual display and every projected image, statistical table or
graphical chart was to be installed on the university web
site. Neither the university administrators nor Alice
expected it to be easy. Changing the technology was the

17

easy part; changing the behavior of the professors who would be required to use the technology was the hard part.

Behavioral change can be a painful process, even when the change is voluntary. This change was not. The professors might be expected to dislike the idea, and they did. They wouldn't listen to anything said about it or read anything written about it. They wouldn't accept it and they wouldn't discuss it, except to grumble. Their resistance was exceeded only by the ways they found to demonstrate their resistance.

They cited scheduling conflicts. Their calendars were booked solid, so jammed and uncoordinated with those of other professors that meetings called to discuss the project were difficult to arrange and sparsely attended.

They pleaded lack of time. Their clocks were maxed out and their bodies were burned out. There simply were not enough hours in the day to manage their class load and accomplish their other associated duties. It was impossible to add the technology project to the mix.

They posed professional arguments. Their instructional material belonged to them. They designed it, they wrote it, and it was their intellectual property. If it went online, others would steal their ideas and claim credit. Why, going online was practically inciting professional piracy, perhaps even inviting plagiarism.

When university administrators continued to advocate for the project, the professors trotted out the mundane excuse everyone uses when resisting change: Things are okay now; why mess with a good thing? If it ain't broke, don't fix it.

But there was no holding back the future. University administrators forced the decision and the word went out; the project was on. Whether anyone liked it or not, whether anyone cooperated or not, Alice had to make it happen. She was a professional; she was responsible for gaining support for her projects, wasn't she?

When the professors—twelve resentful, unwilling, uncooperative men—assembled in the conference room, Alice was the only woman present. The tension was palpable. She noticed it, of course, and she was not surprised. Like other women in leadership roles, she had cut her professional teeth on similar situations. At least she had not been introduced as "our little vase of flowers," as had one of her women colleagues in a similar situation—an apparent compliment that had the effect of minimizing her professionalism while dehumanizing her person.

Alice began. "I will make this transition as smooth as possible for you," she told the professors. "I will give you as much assistance as possible. If you like, I will even come to your office and work individually with you," she promised. Silently, she told herself it was nothing personal that one man refused to sit at the table, choosing instead to sit outside the group in a chair against the wall. The parallel did not escape Alice. His professional back *was* against the wall.

And so were the professional backs of the others. They would change, of course, because they had no choice. But they would change grudgingly. She knew it and they knew it. She would drag them kicking and screaming through the process and they would throw roadblocks up at every turn, making things difficult and unnecessarily prolonging everybody's agony—not because Alice was a woman and they were men, but because that is the nature of organizational change.

Now safely in the familiarity of her own bedroom, physically exhausted and emotionally drained, Alice's frustration bubbled over. Tossing her attaché bag onto the bed, she threw down her professionalism as she threw up her hands in exasperation. "I give up," she announced to the empty room.

Suddenly—whoosh, whoosh—Alice heard two sounds, like two swift inhalations of breath. She felt it immediately and she knew it unmistakably. God the Father and God the Son had entered her body.

For a brief instant, one heavenly instant, it was as if she ceased to exist. Dead yet incomprehensibly alive, she had no boundaries, no limitations, no constraints. Completely capable of thought and intensely aware of absolute freedom, all of Alice's negative feelings—frustration, anger, apprehension, sadness, bitterness—slipped out of her mind like an egg out of a broken shell. *Alice doesn't live here anymore*, she thought, no pun intended. She had heard someone—a minister, perhaps?—define God as Ultimate Reality, and now Alice understood. Her mental clarity was absolute, her material world crisp and clean with no fuzzy edges and no blurry lines. Ultimate Reality was here, present within her.

Was that what it meant to be "slain in the Spirit," she wondered later? No, she had not fainted, had not fallen to the floor, and had not entered a trance. Was it, then, an indwelling of the Holy Spirit? "No," Alice always replied to those who later suggested it, "the Holy Spirit was already with me, and still is. This was the Father and Jesus."

Alice was not confused about what had happened, but she did wonder why. It was a normal question, if not an original one. Jesus' disciples had wondered the same thing.

"Why do you show yourself to your disciples and not to the world?" one of them had asked.

"If anyone loves me," Jesus had replied, "he will obey my teaching. My father will love him, and we will come to him and make our home with him."

Alice loved Jesus. Although she made no claim of perfect obedience to his teaching, she sincerely worked at it and prayed for help in achieving it. This apparently met the biblical criteria Jesus had described.

Alice's bad day at the office had set the stage, and her "I give up"—more a venting of pent-up frustration than a statement of intent—had pronounced the cue. Who would have anticipated the entrance of the Almighty? Certainly not Alice.

No, she would not give up. She had been the grateful recipient of a holy visit—an unexpected, unsolicited, wholly surprising dual visit from God the Father and God the Son. And she would not give up.

- -

At the request of the contributor, the names used in this story are fictitious. The negative feelings Alice had about the university project never returned and she successfully led the professors through the automation process. The holy guests who came to visit Alice took up permanent residence, increasing her awareness that she is never alone.

Wings

The owl will nest there and lay eggs, she will
hatch them, and care for her young under
the shadow of her wings....
Isaiah 34:15

She knew nothing about Isaiah's owl, so Vivian didn't know she cared for people under the shadow of her wings the way Isaiah's owl cared for her young. She thought she was just doing what had to be done.

Even now, years after Kathy's death, Vivian's eyes sometimes filled with tears when she talked about her daughter. From her Vivian had learned much. Love. Enthusiasm. Joy. Quick anger. Easy laughter. Childlike simplicity that came and never left. For Kathy never advanced beyond the mental age of three.

When doctors confirmed the mental disability that Vivian already knew was present, she raged inwardly. Why, God, why? The answer never came, and finally, she stopped asking. It didn't matter, anyway. If she knew why, it would change nothing.

Caring for a three-year-old in the body of an adult for years on end was not the life Vivian had imagined for herself. Now she had to imagine a different life. She had to imagine how strong a three-year-old in a woman's body would be when she became angry or scared. She had to imagine how frightened a three-year-old in a woman's body would be when her first monthly appeared. She had to imagine how vulnerable a three-year-old in a woman's body would be when her hormones began to rage as she reached puberty. She had to imagine—

Vivian could not imagine all the eventualities ahead for Kathy, and whatever was ahead for Kathy was ahead for Vivian. She was a mother; she would do what had to be done. Mothers take care of their children, and if their children have special needs, mothers take care of those, too. Kathy was special, but then again, she wasn't. She was just a regular part of the family, the same way Ken, Vivian's husband was, and the same way David, their firstborn was.

One day when Kathy was about 11, Vivian's next-door neighbor invited Vivian to church. "Thank you, Margaret," said Vivian. "But where would Kathy go?"

Margaret had never thought about it. How could parents of a child with a mental disability go to church if it had no place for the child? And where could a child with a mental disability go to learn about Jesus? Margaret went to her pastor, posed the questions, and the pastor invited Vivian to speak to the church members about the need for a ministry to developmentally disabled people.

On the night of the meeting, the room was full and Margaret sat near the front beaming encouraging smiles at Vivian, who was straightforward, passionate, and painfully honest. It would not be easy to offer a ministry to people with developmental disabilities, some who would require one-on-one assistance. Many needs would have to be addressed, many volunteers involved. "If you decide to do it, do it," Vivian said. "But do *not* do it unless you can do it with joy." The vote was unanimous to proceed. Within a year, the Special Friends Ministry was born with Margaret and her friend Gail its first leaders, and Kathy its first member—its first and *only* member. Until Miss Patty came.

Miss Patty was in her 50s and her mental disability extended back to early childhood. She lived with her grandmother, whose advancing years had begun to make it difficult for her to care for Miss Patty. Grandmother was overwhelmed. What was to become of Miss Patty?

"I'll take care of her," said Vivian, drawing Miss Patty under the shadow of her wings. "Get someone else to handle her financial affairs. I want nothing to do with controlling her money. All I want is to be responsible for her person."

With pro bono legal assistance provided by attorneys who were members of the church, Vivian did what had to be done. She became Miss Patty's guardian, assuming responsibility and authority over her care and custody while Miss Patty continued to live with Grandmother.

Nothing about it was easy, but Vivian became adept at juggling her roles: wife, mother, homemaker, caregiver of Kathy, guardian of Miss Patty, fulltime businessperson, and employer-supervisor of a caregiver for Kathy while Vivian was at work.

Kathy seemed happy with the arrangement. She understood more words than she could speak, and she communicated enthusiastically, especially to Vivian and others who made the effort to learn "Kathy language"—the unique combination of signs and sounds she used to express her wants and needs. Kathy contentedly spent hours in her favorite rocking chair enjoying her two favorite activities: stringing colorful beads and brushing the hair of her dolls, which she collected over the years as birthday and Christmas gifts.

Then David's youthful marriage fell apart and his wife took custody of their little Sara. One day when Sara was three years old, her mother took her to a babysitter and never came back. "Come and get Sara," said the babysitter who phoned David. He did, and struggled to arrange for Sara's care while he worked a fulltime job.

"Bring Sara to me," said Vivian. Soon Sara was living with Vivian and Ken, and soon Vivian had confirmed what she had suspected earlier. Sara never talked. She smiled when Vivian looked her in the eyes and smiled, she walked with assurance, she was clear about her likes and dislikes, and she did many things typical of three-year-olds. Why did Sara have no oral language? Vivian, keenly aware of signs of disabilities, thought she knew, but she needed confirmation. Yes, said the audiologist who tested her; Sara had a hearing loss—86 percent. And it was permanent.

Now the woman who did what had to be done had three people with special needs under the shadow of her wings.

Plunging ahead, Vivian had Sara fitted with hearing aids and arranged for the specialized help necessary to help her acquire speaking skills. Sara's speech developed rapidly, and when it later became clear that she had a learning disability, Vivian and Ken borrowed money for the extra services their granddaughter needed beyond those provided in the public school system or covered by David's financial support.

Meanwhile, Kathy's physical health was failing. Now in her mid-30s, she had survived three terrifying bouts of pneumonia. Vivian had a hospital bed brought into Kathy's room so she could sleep in an upright position. This helped keep the fluid from collecting in her lungs, but her health continued to decline. "We are like two people in the same skin," Vivian said to Kathy's doctors as she interpreted Kathy's needs to them.

One day, Kathy's caregiver phoned Vivian at work. "Kathy is freaking me out," said the caregiver. "Something is wrong." Vivian rushed home to find Kathy animatedly pointing toward a corner of the living room and making excited sounds. As enthused as Kathy was, she was not upset. Throughout the next few days, she occasionally behaved the same way, leaning forward in her rocking chair and reaching both arms straight out to the corner, the way she excitedly reached for a new doll when someone brought her a gift.

It's almost as if there is a doll in the corner, thought Vivian. Nothing excited Kathy like getting a new doll with long hair to brush, unless it was spotting a wigged mannequin—a big doll—in a store. Vivian more than once had removed Kathy from a situation because she had made a beeline for a mannequin to reach for her hair. It was the same at Christmastime when the church displayed life-sized figures of angels with long flowing hair.

Hair. Angels. Angel hair. "Aha! Kathy is seeing angels," said the woman who understood her daughter as if they were in the same skin. And Vivian was certain: If angels were hovering around Kathy, they were preparing to receive her. "I don't think she'll be with us much longer," said Vivian to the caregiver.

Shortly afterward, at age 37, Kathy passed from this world to the next, a casualty of her fourth and final bout with pneumonia. Her vision of the angels had foreshadowed her passing and now she was in a better place. Finally, she was whole.

Life is about loving and letting go. Vivian got the loving part; now she had to get the letting-go part. If anyone had asked her, she would have said she got the letting-go part long ago when she let go of her dreams of hosting all-girl sleepovers, shopping for prom gowns, and greeting wedding guests as mother of the bride.

But that time, her loss had been offset by the privilege of mothering Kathy. This time there was no offset, and now Vivian knew she was wrong. She had not gotten the letting-go part. This time, the anguish lurking behind the years of struggle rushed her like Katrina rushing the levees of New Orleans, ripping loose her underpinnings and leaving her awash in grief. Time after time, she wept her tears and dried them, her sadness waxing and waning like the phases of the moon as the pages of the calendar turned. Then Vivian did what had to be done. She adjusted to life without Kathy, and eventually, she was able to celebrate Kathy's life as much as she mourned her death.

Today, Kathy's legacy as founding member of the Special Friends Ministry is an enduring presence in its ongoing operations. If asked, Vivian would not say she cared for people under the shadow of her wings the way Isaiah's owl cared for her young. She would say she did what had to be done. Some say they are the same.

- -

Miss Patty, who died in 1998, spent her last years in a group home after Grandmother died. Sara, who graduated from high school in 2000, is self-supporting as an aide in a classroom of autistic children. The Special Friends Ministry of Fredericksburg Baptist Church, which co-founders Margaret Ingram and Gail Hylton call a transformative experience for the church, has grown until 30 years later, it includes two residential group homes owned by the church and operated in cooperation with Hopetree Ministries, where Mrs. Hylton (see "Arms") is Area Coordinator. Vivian West, manager of Bejeweled Designs in historic Fredericksburg, Virginia, is still drawing people under the shadow of her wings; see "Feather."

Feather

Give me a sign of your goodness...for you, O Lord,
have helped me and comforted me.
Psalm 86:17

She wasn't looking for the bridge between earth and heaven that day. And when she found it, she didn't know exactly what it was. At first, it looked like only a feather—a dark wing feather about three inches long. It seemed out of place in the small gift boutique, but it wasn't. It was exactly where it meant to be: on a mission to find Vivian.

The boutique, its single aisle stretching about 50 feet from front to back, had been closed for the night, and Vivian only moments earlier had unlocked it for the business day. How could the feather have traveled all the way to the back of the shop, even if somehow it had blown in through the open front door?

Perhaps when Vivian reached for the feather she disturbed the air around it. Perhaps an indiscernible draft was flowing across the floor. Whatever the cause, the feather somehow slid underneath the counter and out of sight. Vivian turned toward the closet for a broom and her inner voice spoke. *Don't throw the feather away*, it said.

Vivian knew her inner voice well. God lived within her (John 14:17), and his spirit sometimes spoke to her silently. She had learned to tell the difference between her inner voice and her own thought. Her thought would have been, "I'm not going to throw the feather away"; the emphasis would have been on what she herself had decided. But the words "Don't throw the feather away" were instructions from another source.

28

No, she would not throw the feather away; she would keep it. But first, she had to retrieve it from underneath the counter. Broom in hand, she returned to the spot, and unbelievably, there lay the feather. Somehow, in the few seconds it took Vivian to go to the broom closet and return, the feather had moved back out in front of the counter.

Tape the feather inside the cover of your copy of "The Shack,"[6] said Vivian's inner voice. Use strong tape so the feather will not be lost. Apply the tape to the quill, leaving the plume free but safe from harm. When you finish the book, give it to Claire Ann in exchange for her copy, leaving her with the book that has the feather inside.

The message made perfect sense to Vivian. Claire Ann had been her good friend since coming to work with her after Vivian's daughter died. Kathy's death had been very difficult for Vivian, and five years later, she had begun to see that God had a special reason to bring Claire Ann into her life. For one recent starry night while walking across a high bridge, Claire Ann's 22-year-old son had accidentally fallen to his death.

As distraught as Vivian was when Kathy died, that's how distraught Claire Ann was when Graham died. Why, God, why? Graham had much to offer the world. He was a good person, a creative and talented artist. Losing him was like losing a part of herself.

Vivian understood and so did God, for the instruction to tape the feather inside the cover of *The Shack* and give it to Claire Ann was not the first message Vivian's inner voice had given her for Claire Ann. The first message was the poem.

One morning when Vivian opened the gift boutique for business, the poem had popped into her mind like popcorn in a popper. She was not a poet, but her inner voice was, and it had given her several inspirational poems that a graphics artist had transformed into colorful greeting cards sold in the boutique. Vivian hurried to the back of the shop to grab a pencil and write the words while they were fresh in her mind:

> He was a bright and rising star
> I can see his reflection in your eyes
> Now he runs across the night
> His magic lights up the skies.

Vivian knew the poem was meant for Claire Ann, and when Vivian gave it to her, another friend interpreted it. People could see Graham reflected in Claire Ann's eyes, said the friend, because mother and son were mirror images of each other. They were close when he was in this world and they were close now when she turned her thoughts to the nighttime heaven, where Graham's spirit shines like a star. The validity of the poem was affirmed when the background of "A Star is Born," a portrait of Graham painted and titled by an artist who had a photo of Graham but had never read or heard of the poem, displayed a bridge underneath a starry nighttime sky.

And what about *The Shack*? Vivian had started to read the novel and had introduced Claire Ann to it. The setting is a shack where Mack, who is grieving the death of his daughter, meets God, engages him in dialogue, and sees his daughter happy in heaven. In the course of Mack's encounter with God, the grieving father's faith and his concept of God are destroyed and rebuilt on a healthier foundation, and he leaves the shack a man changed for the better. Vivian and Claire Ann often discussed the surprise bestseller, sharing their thoughts and comparing Mack's experience with their own.

As for the feather, many ancient peoples considered birds, at home in the space between earth and heaven, a little closer to God than other earthly creatures. Native American chiefs wore feathers to symbolize their communion with Spirit. Celtic Druids wore feathers to help them gain knowledge of the celestial realm. In literary terms, the feather is a metaphor for the soul. Regardless of the culture or the era, birds shed their feathers and new ones grow in their place, so the feather symbolizes new life after death and spiritual ascension to a higher existence.

What could better represent the relationship of the two women whose ascended offspring now bound their mothers together like birds of a feather? What could better represent Graham's ascended spirit? Unlike the psalmist, Vivian had not asked for a sign of God's goodness, but he had sent it, and the woman God had comforted in the loss of her daughter was now a part of God's plan to comfort Claire Ann in the loss of her son.

Yes, Graham, thought Vivian, looking skyward, *I will stay close to your mother and care for her.* Then she wrote in her copy of *The Shack:* "To Vivian from Graham for Graham's Mom," taped the feather on the inside cover, and exchanged books with Claire Ann. No one except Vivian and Claire Ann would understand the meaning of the inscription, but then, no one else needed to understand.

Today Vivian draws comfort from the promise of Jesus: "Because I live, you also will live" (John 14:19, NIV). She looks forward to reuniting with Kathy someday, and at times, she feels she already has. Because one day she found a feather and now she knows. The feather of spirit is the bridge between earth and heaven.

- -- -

Claire Ann Stevenson and Vivian West, manager of Bejeweled Designs, Fredericksburg, Virginia, entered "The Shack" and came out changed for the better. The account of Vivian's experience with her daughter is told in "Wings."

Guest

The Lord is my shepherd, I shall not be in want.
Psalm 23:1

Divorce shouted. At first barely audible in the distance, it swelled in crescendo as it advanced, its cadence ending in cruel childish singsong:

> Nya, nya, nya-nya, nya,
> Robert left Beth
> She's lost her lover
> Robert's out the gate
> He loves another.
> Nya, nya, nya-nya, nya....

Beth hated divorce, detested the very idea of it. She had always thought divorce was for people who ignored the needs of their spouse, or abdicated their commitment, or refused to seek out counselors who could help them see a different option. None of these conditions fit Beth's case. She had catered to Robert's needs, had reaffirmed her commitment to him, and had gone for professional counseling. Still, Robert was determined to have his divorce and it seemed nothing Beth could do or say could stop it.

How well she remembered their first meeting. "Beth," Carole had said, "come to dinner and meet Robert. I met him at church and he asked if I knew any single women."

Now bumping into her middle years, content in her singleness and happy in her career in church ministry, Beth was a bit dubious. But she went to Carole's home and met this gray-haired man of the crinkly blue eyes, this business man who had relocated to northern Virginia for a job with the US government, this man eager to make new friends.

It was hardly a successful evening. Robert talked incessantly, monopolized the conversation, and came across as smug, arrogant, and self-absorbed. Recognizing a disaster in the making, Carole tried in vain to bring Beth into the conversation.

If lies are the lubricant of social discourse, truth is sand in its gears. Having nothing to lose, Beth laid her napkin beside her plate, folded her hands in her lap, and dumped a full load of sand. "You are the most egotistical, conceited, rudest man I have ever met," she said softly, looking Robert straight in the eyes.

The moment was as surreal as a clock melting and dripping off the edge of a table in a Salvadore Dali painting. Carole was speechless, Robert dumbfounded. "I—uh—I don't understand," he stammered.

The last drip of the clock splattered on the floor. "I have spent the entire evening with you, and not once did you show the slightest interest in me, or in Carole, for that matter. Not once did you show that it matters to you what I think or feel about anything, where I come from, what I like or don't like. Not once did you show any concern about anyone or anything but yourself," Beth said, holding Robert's eyes in a steady gaze.

"I—" he faltered, "I didn't realize—"

"Well, realize!" Beth replied, keeping her tone soft. Then she rose from the table and walked toward the door, Carole and Robert rising to follow her. "I'll see myself out," Beth said, closing the door behind her.

Silence ballooned as the nightmare of the guest became the horror of the hostess. Carole, secretly proud of Beth, shrugged her shoulders. "Well, at least she didn't slug you," she finally managed.

"No, but she might as well have. The thing is, I'm afraid she's right. Do you think she'll kill me if I call her tomorrow? Not tonight—tomorrow."

"If she had wanted to kill you she would have killed you already," said Carole. "But do call; an apology is always in order. Just leave me out of it. You're on your own now."

Robert made a hasty exit, too embarrassed to remember to thank his hostess for the evening. Carole leaned against the closed door and sighed. *This is why friends who want to stay friends don't fix them up,* she thought, swearing off matchmaking forever.

The next day, Carole phoned Beth and apologized for setting her up with an egoist. "That's okay, you couldn't have known," said Beth as gracious as ever. They left it there, Carole thankful that it takes more than one bad evening to spoil a real friendship.

It took Robert more than a day to work up his nerve; it took a week. Then he phoned Beth and hurriedly delivered his prepared speech. First, he apologized; he now saw his mistake. He had felt uncomfortable in the social setting and had overcompensated by talking too much. It wasn't an excuse, just an explanation, but he would be grateful for a chance to start over.

A mistake of self-consciousness, Beth thought. Wanting but also fearing the stereotypical fix-up, Robert had considered Beth a quality inspector out to reject him for the slightest flaw and any gap in conversation a culprit out to expose that flaw. Talking was a self-conscious defense mechanism, an ineffective one that brought about the very rejection Robert feared.

"It's too late to start over," Beth told him. "But we can start again." So they did, Robert the Second replacing Robert the First. Robert the Second was a good conversationalist—considerate, well read, and intelligent. As they became better acquainted, he became tender, caring, and romantic. They fell in love and a year later, they married.

At first good, the marriage soon began a downward slide. Over the next few years, it moved through various stages of painful conflict and distressing isolation until it was not good. Not good at all. Beth approached these changes with a mixture of confusion and prayer, genuinely trying to work things out and finally persuading Robert to go with her for marriage counseling. Efforts at problem resolution failed, however, and Robert, who months earlier had secretly chosen Beth's replacement, took his personal belongings and moved in with the other woman.

Beth's very fragile marriage had come apart at its very fragile seams.

Alone one morning at the kitchen table, Beth sat looking out the window at the small backyard garden. Like a woman mentioned in the Bible, Beth was a married woman unloved (Proverbs 30:21-23). How could she bear it? Robert was resisting any financial support for her, and she could not survive on her part-time ministry salary that was too small to pay a mortgage, much less utilities, insurance, and other expenses. She wondered about working fulltime again, even if she could find fulltime work in her field. In unbearable pain and afraid for her future, even her body hurt. She felt like dying.

The Psalms had always comforted Beth when nothing else did. She opened her Good News Bible and instinctively turned to Psalm 23, verse 1, and this time, she understood the words as never before. The Lord was her Shepherd and she had all she needed! Beth had always thought of that verse as a promise: *Someday* she would have everything she needed. But it wasn't a promise; it was a declaration. She *already* had all she needed. "I have all I need and all I need is the Lord," Beth said aloud.

Suddenly, an altered state of reality overcame her, an intense awareness in which every cell in her body and every scintilla of her mind came alive to a Presence that she could not see but physically felt. Instantly, Beth knew. God was beside her at the table, the area where he sat charged with a radiant energy more real than from a human being and as recognizable as the presence of someone else is to a blind person.

In the presence of this holy guest, the burden slipped from Beth's shoulders and lay in a shriveled heap on the floor, impotent and abandoned. Then her guest slipped away, leaving her confident that the one who had come to her in the kitchen would go with her to the courtroom, if necessary, and from there to wherever life would take her.

Divorce. Beth had run from it, hid from it, fought it. She didn't ask for it, didn't seek it, didn't want it. But when she couldn't stop it, the good Shepherd came to guide her through it. And he was all she needed.

- -

In a startling turn of events, a heart attack following a surgical procedure took Robert's life before the divorce was final. Beth Hayworth Echols could have been the widow Timothy mentioned who prayed day and night asking God for help (I Timothy 5:5). A Christian counselor guided Beth through her shock and loss, and with the support of a loving church family, her career opportunities greatly expanded. Today she praises God that she has everything she needs—even a loving and faithful second husband.

Wind

He makes the clouds his chariot and rides on the
wings of the wind. He makes winds his
messengers....
Psalm 104:3b-4a

The Devil's Breath was taking a breather. It had tired itself out blowing up a firestorm last year and now the notorious wind was just a breeze lazily easing through the canyons. Joe and Lisa didn't notice. They were planning a church retreat at the beach and they were listening to God, not the wind.

At first, Lisa hadn't planned to go. Married a mere seven and a half years, life now was radically different from life at Virginia Tech where she and Joe had met at their campus church and fallen in love. It had been a big decision to leave family, friends, and the spectacular foothills of the Shenandoahs to move to the West coast, but the newlywed Raceks had the best of reasons. They had heard a call to plant neighborhood churches in Los Angeles with Great Commission Ministries and had responded in faith.

Life was both rewarding and stressful. Committed wife of a young pastor and stay-at-home mother of four children ages six and under, Lisa keenly felt her responsibility. The children were in constant motion, every waking moment at least one of them demanding her attention. She found little down time, and if a camping trip to the beach seemed more like work than relaxation to Lisa, Joe understood. The decision was easy. Lisa would stay at home and spend a little one-on-one time with two-year-old Tyler while Joe rode with another family and took Dawson, Katie, and Will to the retreat.

But the next day, rested and relaxed, Lisa changed her mind. It was mid-October on the Pacific coast of California and a tent on the beach was inviting. How could she turn down the bright sun and singing surf, the salt sea air and spontaneous laughter? She couldn't.

Packing an overnight bag with a few extra clothes and her sunscreen, Lisa grabbed some books and toys, threw them into the family minivan, and strapped Tyler into his car seat. Listening to a tape about glorifying God in the little daily chores of life, Lisa and Tyler enjoyed the hour's drive down the Pacific Coast Highway to join the rest of the family. It was a good day; God was on his throne and all was well.

Every year, the hot Santa Ana winds sweep across southern California in late fall and winter. The winds, strong and dry, can combine with climatic heat and drought to turn the prevailing dense thickets of bushes and small trees into explosive fuel that feeds the legendary wildfires for which the region is well known. Named for the Santa Ana canyons, the winds rip through the mountain passes, picking up speed as they go and generating warnings from state officials that no one may start an outdoor fire lest the Devil's Breath turn a spark from a lighted match or an outdoor grill into a raging inferno.

When Lisa and Tyler arrived at the campsite, the wind had picked up a bit but it was pleasant, not nearly as strong as the day before. Joe was proud of their tent, and just as proud that he had found it for a bargain price on craigslist.com, which billed it as large enough to sleep nine adults. It now sheltered two families—the Raceks and the Coopers—providing sleeping quarters for two couples and their children by night, and quiet space for the naps of seven children by day.

The entire experience was a delight. The group, including co-pastor Andy Blevins and his family, numbered about 40 people in several tents. The children chased seagulls and dug in the sand. The families played active games together and enjoyed food prepared without benefit of a microwave. They didn't miss the world of technology; cell phones were for emergencies only. No video games with their wild cartoon characters. No televisions with their artificial laugh tracks. No emails demanding immediate response. If the young adults noticed how much like their own parents they had become, concerned about how fast the world is changing and determined to teach their children to appreciate old-fashioned values of God, home, and country, they didn't mention it.

For people who live in a city where artificial light washes the nighttime sky with a yellowish tinge that renders the stars invisible to the naked eye, the biggest treat was looking up and searching out the constellations. With the rumble of the Los Angeles traffic far away and only the peaceful sound of waves lapping the shore, the mystery of God's creation was inescapable. Perhaps they were feeling exactly how the psalmist felt, thought the young families as they prayed together and read the Bible: "The heavens declare the glory of God; the skies proclaim the work of his hands" (Psalm 19:1, NIV).

A little after midnight, lying in bed strangely awake, Joe felt a physical restlessness overtaking him and a persistent thought dogging his mind: He should collect his family and take them home. He tried to dismiss the idea, telling himself he was being foolish. Everybody was safely bedded down. It would be unnecessarily disruptive to wake them and drive home. The children would be grouchy and uncooperative, the commotion in the middle of the night would disturb the other families, and Joe would have to drive back to the camp the next day to lead the retreat devotional. Still, his restlessness nagged him.

"Lisa," he whispered, touching her gently on the shoulder. "Are you awake?"

"Yes," she murmured, raising her head. "I can't sleep with all this wind."

Just as I thought, the wind is keeping Lisa awake. Then he told her what he was thinking.

Lisa could have resisted, could have complained that she had just gotten there and she might as well not have come if they were going home now, but she didn't. "I'm willing to stay," she said agreeably, "but we'll do whatever you think best."

Resting but not asleep, Joe lay in the dark, the nagging thought draping his mind like a damp towel on a bathroom floor, out of place and completely inexcusable. Thirty minutes later, he still could not pick up the towel. Quietly he crept among the shadows to Andy's side. "Hey, Andy," he whispered, waking his friend. "I hate to bother you, but I need to take my family home."

"Okay, man," whispered the co-pastor. "No problem. I'll stay here and finish things up." Feeling as odd as they were determined, Joe and Lisa collected their things, roused the children and drove home, the wind rudely nudging their van along the way.

Fifteen minutes later, the Devil's Breath raged across the camp, ripping Joe and Lisa's tent apart at the seams, breaking support poles and collapsing the tent on top of the Coopers. Frantically, they literally fought their way out of the flapping shreds of canvas. Sand stinging their eyes, the parents struggled to comfort their crying children during the repeat trips back and forth to the car to stash their belongings.

Throughout the night, like an army of blow dryers in revolt, hot gusts of wind measuring up to 111 miles per hour split the tents apart one by one, bending some support poles and snapping others as if they were toothpicks. The families, unharmed and led by co-pastor Andy, collected their gear and abandoned the campsite.

The next week a series of wildfires swept across southern California. Whipped by the Santa Ana winds, the fires of October 2007 destroyed 1,500 homes and charred over 500,000 acres before burning out 19 days later, killing 9 people and injuring 85.

When it was all over, Joe knew his restlessness had been the urging of God and his nagging thought God's still small voice. Like Elijah, Joe had heard God's gentle whisper, except that Joe heard it before a fire and Elijah heard it after (I Kings 19:12-14). But why did God lead Joe and his family away from the storm and leave the other campers in it? The answer lies in the outcome. God protected all of them, and in the process, they trusted him, the co-pastors trusted each other, and the people trusted the leadership of both co-pastors.

In the 1960s, Marshall McLuhan's *The Medium is the Massage* argued that the dominant communication medium shapes the way people think and act as much as does the message itself. McLuhan may not have had the Devil's Breath in mind as a communication medium, but that's what God had in mind when he jumped into his cloud chariot and rode on the wings of the wind. And when he made the wind his messenger, Joe and Lisa heard him—and obeyed. Because they listened to God *and* the wind.

Wind

- -

At the time of these events, Joe and Lisa Racek were part of the pastoral team of Kairos Los Angeles, a network of interdenominational Christian churches in west Los Angeles and Hollywood. The Raceks have since relocated to the mountains of Virginia to continue their ministry in Blacksburg's New Life Christian Fellowship, the church where they met.

Tears

*When Jesus saw her weeping...he was deeply moved
in spirit and troubled...Jesus wept.*
John 11:33-35

The last seven weeks were not normal. Anything that seemed normal was a hoax, an aberration that showed up at Sabrina's door masquerading as normalcy and convincing no one. At least not Sabrina.

Now after her C-section that morning, the masquerade was over and night was upon her. The darkness had not come soon enough, so eager was she to adorn herself in its well-known cloak and pour out her brokenness to God. But words would not come.

Her baby would be disabled, doctors had told Sabrina weeks ago. Nevertheless, she had hoped for the best. So when the baby's little heart stopped two hours after she was born, Sabrina's heart shattered. Its serrated edges now lay as rough and jagged within her chest as the incision line lay smooth and even on her belly. Now alone in her hospital room with nothing to do but think, Sabrina was wordless— a nebulous amorphous blob of confusion and uncertainty.

It would be several months before physicians would explain little Beatrice Marie's death: an incomplete nervous system. All Sabrina knew was that she was exhausted and uncomfortable, her arms overflowing with the emptiness of loss, her embrace as vacant as her mood was dark.

"We'll be back tomorrow," Betty had said, bending to give her daughter a hug before leaving. It was a familiar routine, people saying goodbye at Sabrina's bedside and leaving her to a painfully sleepless night.

During the last seven weeks of her difficult pregnancy when Sabrina had been confined to bed, she had developed mixed feelings about the night. As grateful as she had been for the friends from her church who came daily to her home to do things that she temporarily was unable to do for her family, she had often felt overwhelmed by the constant presence of others. She had come to look forward to the night when everyone left except her husband and their three children, and they were all upstairs safely asleep. Still, the loneliness at three o'clock in the morning could be oppressive.

Despite its tyrannical loneliness—or perhaps because of it—Sabrina had learned that God was more real at night than at any other time. The day held many distractions—conversations, duties, needs. It was hard for Sabrina to notice God during the day, even though she knew he was present.

But in the thick quiet of night when Sabrina was in pain and could not sleep, she often noticed God, and could pray and read the Bible with ease as at no other time. God was with her, always available, even when the rest of her world was asleep. She always had words for God then.

Now the night was upon her again, the night of the anguished day she had welcomed her baby daughter into the world and kissed her goodbye two hours later. Guiltily, almost impatiently, Sabrina had waited for them to leave—her parents, her siblings, her husband, and his parents—coveting the time when she could turn to God in the familiar solitude of night. But unexplainably, now in the hours of darkness Sabrina had sought, she had no words.

Great sadness overtook her then—pure, unbounded, unfettered sadness—raging over her like an avalanche down a mountain, crushing and unstoppable. Gathering strength as it gobbled up her sagging spirit, it clutched the fragments of her shattered heart in its bony fingers, ground the shards into dust, and puffed the particles into her lungs, where they infiltrated her bloodstream and engulfed her from within. The anger would come later. Right now, there was only sadness—menacing, debilitating, pernicious sadness. Sabrina began to cry, unable to stem the tide and ashamed of herself for crying again after a day filled with weeping.

That was when God came. Wrapping his arms around her, he held her close, the way a father holds a child. Cuddling her against his chest, his heartbeat throbbed against her cheek as he gently rocked her side to side, soothing her aching spirit. *He is not ashamed of my tears, even if I am.* Then he began to weep, his tears mingling with Sabrina's as they ran down her face and fell onto her hospital gown. Not only was he unashamed of her tears, he was shedding his own tears. But unlike Sabrina, he was not weeping *for* his daughter; he was weeping *with* his daughter.

A few short moments passed. Seconds? A minute? As Sabrina's tears subsided, the sense of God's arms around her faded and she remembered the story in the gospel of John. Just as Jesus had gone to the grieving family of Lazarus and wept with them, God had come to this grieving mother and wept with her.

Sabrina was still sad and her arms were still empty. She was still hospitalized and she was still sore from surgical wound. She still had long, slow grief work to do and she still had no words. But now she needed none. For when she had no words, God had heard her tears.

- -

Sabrina Culley Justison, of Elkton, Maryland, stays busy mothering and home schooling her children. Sabrina is the daughter of Betty Phillips Culley, whose perspective on Sabrina's pregnancy and the baby's birth and death is told in "Rain."

Rain

*Let my teaching fall like rain and my words descend
like dew, like showers on new grass, like abundant
rain on tender plants.*
Deuteronomy 32:2

A mother understands what a child does not say. If the proverb had not predated Betty, it could have been written especially for her. She had learned the lesson from her own mother, a young widow who struggled to bring up her two daughters on her meager earnings as a dressmaker and postal clerk in a worked-out mining village in Kentucky. Now living in Delaware, Betty lived out her mother's love every day. Especially today.

Elbows on knees and arms wrapped around her shoulders in a subconscious gesture of self-comfort, Betty sat puzzled in the hospital waiting room. Although she had long been a Christian, now she could not pray. Although she had long been a journal keeper, now she could not write. *How strange that I have no words,* thought Betty. Her mind wandered to her troubled daughter, and then to how Sabrina had come to her in the first place.

Betty had met Jerry in the late 1950s when he was one of The Four J's, college buddies who coined the term for their informal foursome. Joe, Jack, and another Jerry fixed Jerry and Betty up, and then stood back and smiled over the weeks and months as the young couple fell in love. After Jerry's graduation, he and Betty married and produced three daughters, who subsequently produced the next generation: seven grandchildren.

It was now 1994. Jerry and Betty had contentedly settled into middle age, happy with each other and their family. Just before Christmas, they learned that their youngest daughter was pregnant with her fourth child. Jerry and Betty were thrilled, especially when Sabrina's rapidly expanding abdomen led the doctor to suspect she might be carrying twins. Not so, revealed the ultrasound, just one little girl. Sabrina and her husband named the unborn baby Beatrice Marie, and Jerry and Betty began to dream of another grandchild to love.

Months passed and by June, Sabrina was unusually large. The results of a more extensive ultrasound were frightening but explained her abnormal girth. The baby's joints were not developing properly, making it impossible for her to lie in the fetal position, and she was not swallowing the amniotic fluid, which blocked its normal transfer to Sabrina's kidneys for processing. Beatrice's heart was beating beautifully and her brain was normal, but it was unclear how well her lungs were developing. Sure to be born severely disabled, she would require much physical therapy.

The news was difficult to hear, but Betty immediately took it to God, praying for Sabrina and the baby and asking God to prepare the family so they could provide whatever care mother and baby would need after the birth.

Seven difficult weeks followed. The doctor prescribed complete bed rest for Sabrina, a prescription that seemed impossible to fill, given her husband's daily work schedule and the ages of their children, who were too young to care for themselves.

The news spread quickly throughout Sabrina's church family, who took it as a call to action. They made meals. They fed and bathed the children. They helped Sabrina with the children's home schooling. They cleaned house and ran errands. They completely managed the household, making it possible for Sabrina to stay in bed and earning the family's everlasting gratitude.

Meanwhile, Sabrina was growing larger every day, becoming very uncomfortable and not sleeping. When extreme discomfort graduated to unrelenting pain, doctors considered giving her relief by withdrawing some of the amniotic fluid, but they soon abandoned the idea of the invasive procedure as too risky. They scheduled a Caesarean section for eight o'clock the next morning.

The day dawned thick with clouds, and by eight o'clock, the darkened sky was pouring rain. At eight thirty, their son-in-law entered the hospital waiting room where Betty and Jerry sat. Their eyes searching his in anticipation, the silent question was written on their faces. "She had the baby and Sabrina is doing okay," said the young father quietly, a muscle working in his jaw. "But they can't save the baby." An involuntary gasp escaped Betty's lips. "Her heart is still beating but she's having trouble breathing and her lungs are insufficiently developed for them to ventilate her."

Tears rained down like the torrents outside, hearts as heavy as the lowering clouds that spilled their water on the ground.

The hospital staff allowed Sabrina to keep the baby with her, going to them periodically to check on Sabrina's condition and monitor Beatrice's heartbeat so they could record the exact time of death. The baby's strong little heart would beat for two more hours.

Betty waited and ached. Only those who have lost a baby know how it hurts to lose a newborn, and only another mother knows how Betty agonized for the suffering she would have born for her daughter, but could not. Still, Betty could not pray and could not write.

Finally, the baby was gone.

Is denial stronger than knowledge? Does hope never die in the heart of one who loves God? Is the human spirit endowed with some primeval drive that ever presses for one more second of life, knowing that death can come at any second but believing it won't be *this* second? Whatever the reason, the expected news took Betty by surprise. Looking up, she noticed that the rain was stopping and the sun had appeared. *My skies have been crying with you,* thought Betty. Then she remembered the essence of Romans 8:26: *My Spirit has been speaking on your behalf with groans you could not express.*

Like the sea washing the shore, unexpressed words washed over the battered shoals of Betty's heart. Then the waves receded, leaving in their wake expressed words— honest words, mournful words, therapeutic words; words of loss and sorrow, hope and healing, life and love. Descending like dew, like showers on new grass, words began to fill up Betty's journal with bittersweet release. *Praise the Lord of the brightening skies, whose teaching falls like rain.*

- -

Betty and Jerry Culley are now retired and have downsized into their retirement home in Newark, Delaware. Sabrina's perspective on her baby's birth and death is described in "Tears.

Sunbeam

*The people living in darkness have seen a great
light; on those living in the land of the shadow of
death a light has dawned.*
Matthew 4:16

She sat on a log pondering her quandary, pen and journal
in hand. Mentally comparing herself to Bunyan's pilgrim,
Linda was undeniably slogging around in her own personal
slough of despond.

The last few years, quandary seemed to be her lot, some
important decision always hounding her. She had willingly
adopted her family's expectation that she would earn a
college degree, so that was not an issue. The issues were
what courses to study and what major to pursue. On those
decisions hinged at least one more: what career path to
follow.

The first decisions made, the last one plagued her. It
would be years before she would reflect on the absurdity of
young people making such life-altering decisions when
they have such little life experience to guide them.

Linda was now in the college of her choice taking the
courses of her choice to prepare for the career of her
choice. Social work, she thought. But she wasn't sure.
Brought up in the church, she had been taught that God had
a plan for her life and all would be well if she just followed
the plan. Fine, she was willing. But what was the plan? And
how was she to find it?

As if education and career decisions were not enough,
she was in a blue funk about the world she lived in. Many
good people were doing many good things, yet poverty,
disease and violence abounded. Always, somewhere, a war
was in progress, and other wars were threatened. The

environment was in danger with a hole in the ozone layer, acid in the rain, PCBs in the ground water, and people chopping down the rain forests. This was the world she was supposed to find her way in, find a career in?

Overwhelmed with uncertainty, she looked homeward. Hers was a family of women: her mother, her three sisters, and herself. Linda's father had died when she was 15, so she had firsthand knowledge that not all plans work out the way the planners intend. Her mother had not planned to be a widow at such a young age, but when it became necessary for her to manage her life alone, she did. "Linda," she said when Linda shared her career dilemma, "I don't care what you do. I just want you to be happy."

Still predictably Mother, Linda thought. *If only Daddy were here!* But he was never coming back. How long would it be before she stopped missing him? In this case, it wouldn't have mattered, because in her heart, Linda knew the truth. He would have been like her mother: supportive of whatever decision Linda made but setting no direction for her.

Who would have believed that Linda would long for the days when her parents decided for her? She had only lately come to realize that it was a luxury available only to children and teenagers to blame parents when things did not "work out."

Linda sought out the student religious organization on campus, where the adult leader at least understood young adult angst and where students followed a godly life, even if Linda sometimes did not understand their way of thinking. They spoke a language of Zion laced with phrases lifted from the Bible and augmented by contemporary religious platitudes that sometimes had the unintended effect of excluding those outside the inner circle. "You gotta turn it over," for example. This meant something akin to, "You need to trust God to solve the problem and quit trying to solve it yourself."

It was a fundamentally religious way of talking that others seemed to understand but Linda sometimes didn't—especially the phrase, "It's gonna happen." Others sometimes intoned this phrase during prayer time and Bible study sessions. "It's gonna happen," they would say—meaning something akin to, "God will make things right," or "God will give you the answer and then you'll feel better." But they never defined what "it" was, so how was Linda to know when "it" happened?

"Don't worry," they said when she asked, "you'll just know."

"You mean like when you fall in love?" They looked at her blankly.

Two years in a row, Linda had attended a student retreat at her denomination's state campgrounds, a secluded mountainous area where periods of Bible study, worship, and private devotional time bracketed opportunities for outdoor recreation and free time. Searching for some special insight, she had gone there hoping that her own personal "it" would happen. But two years in a row, she had returned to campus still uncertain about her future, disappointed that the elusive "it" yet evaded her.

Now at her third retreat, the day was overcast and gray, matching the grayness of her spirit. She deserted the group in favor of the solitude of the woods where, even on a bright day, the sun rarely penetrated the thick overhanging canopy of branches. Tramping down a worn path on a cushiony blanket of dropped pine needles and fallen leaves, the forested silence was broken only by the occasional snap of a twig underfoot. The earthy fragrance of damp undergrowth filled her nostrils, a perfect complement to her somber mood. Finding a seat on a downed tree trunk, she placed her open journal on her lap and pondered her quandary. And there she sat.

Finally, an idea came. Maybe "it" was not a specific answer to a specific need at a specific time. "God," she wrote, "I release you from all expectations of making 'it' happen. I accept that you will light my path in your own way and in your own time."

Suddenly, a shaft of sunlight broke through her leafy sanctuary and, with laser-like precision, spotlighted the words she had just written. Startled, she looked skyward. The sun was absent, only one isolated patch of gray sky visible overhead. *The people living in darkness have seen a great light,* she thought. Only this time, the remembered words took on new meaning.

Linda arose and walked out of the woods into the same sunless day, but now there was an important difference. She had entered the woods in confusion; she exited the woods in confidence. Her private struggle was over; God's shining affirmation had verified her insight. For when the light dawned, "it" happened.

- -

Linda Ward followed the light of God's leading into social work, and when the career dilemma began to hound her again, she followed the light of his leading to the seminary. She earned a Master's of Religious Education and was later ordained. At this writing, she serves as Minister of Education at Walnut Hills Baptist Church in Williamsburg, Virginia.

Revision

In the year that King Uzziah died, I saw the Lord
seated on a throne, high and exalted....
Isaiah 6:1

She was eighteen and didn't know what she didn't know. And she didn't know it. What she knew was that she loved Joshua and he loved her. Their marriage, bound in Christian teaching and African tradition, would never end. Somebody else's might, but not theirs.

So why was Carroll here in her father's study asking his permission to move back home?

He had brought her and the rest of his young family to Africa when she was only seven, after he spent years in the West earning his medical degree, doing his residency, and planning his return to his native Nigeria to establish a hospital and practice medicine for the benefit of his own people. Now he listened as his daughter poured out her heart.

"I have no comment about what you say," he responded. "But I will tell you that your aunt and uncle came back from the medicine man in the village six weeks ago and said you would be home in six weeks. And your mother said six weeks ago while she was praying, God told her that you would be home within six weeks. Now here you are."

Carroll was astounded. As surprising as were the earlier events of the day, her father's words were just as surprising. Family members had foreknowledge of what she had not even thought about until that very morning! It was the only confirmation Carroll needed that she had made the right decision. She would leave her husband.

Earlier that day, she and Joshua had attended church together. Well tutored in the scripture, she knew by memory the verse the minister referenced, and she readily turned to it in her Bible. But this time, the words were different, speaking a message tailored just for her and giving her specific direction. Her understanding of that direction was why she now sat in her father's study anxiously awaiting his decision.

"When would you like to move back home?" he asked.

"Today," she said, silently thanking God for Christian parents.

"That's good. If you had said tomorrow or later, I would have known you weren't ready. Your mother and I don't want to pressure you, but we think at 18, you are too young to be married. Go back to your house and pack your things. Your mother will pick you up at six-thirty."

Joshua lay sprawled out on their creaky iron bed when Carroll got home. That morning in the worship service, she had tried to show him the scripture passage, whispering loudly, "Look," and poking his arm with her Bible as she pointed to the words.

But he didn't see. Or couldn't see, or wouldn't. "Shh," he had whispered, placing a finger over his lips to quiet her, embarrassed as other worshippers shot disapproving glances at them.

But he didn't whisper now. "What?" he shouted, leaping off the bed when she announced that she was leaving him.

"Yes, I'm moving back home. Mother will be here at six-thirty to pick me up."

Joshua was incredulous. "You mean today?"

"Yes, today," she said, scrambling to collect her things.

Desperate to stop her, he lobbed questions at her, trying to start a distracting argument. "But I thought you loved me," he finally said. "Don't you love me?"

"Yes," she admitted, directly meeting his eyes. "But I must go."

Rummaging through her dresser, she threw her personal belongings into her bags, unwilling to acknowledge to him what she silently acknowledged to herself. She thought Joshua drank too much and she suspected him of visiting prostitutes when he was out with his male friends. She had made excuses for him, as though his not beating her entitled him to infidelity.

Glancing at the clock, she grabbed her bags and headed out the door. With no regret, no sadness, and no longing—not even when she pushed away fleeting feelings of need for him—she almost skipped down the lane to the dusty road in front of the house. She usually had to run to keep up with long-legged Joshua, but this time he had to run to keep up with her.

Carroll's mother sat at the foot of the hill in her white Renault. Trying to force a lingering embrace as Carroll opened the car door, Joshua pulled her to his chest and whispered in her ear, "Why, Carroll, why?"

It was an appropriate question and he deserved an answer. Someday soon she would tell him what she herself could hardly believe. That morning in church, when she had opened her Bible to the sixth chapter of Isaiah, she had read, "In the year that your marriage dies, you will see the Lord." Blinking, she had looked again, and then had tried to draw Joshua's attention to the words. When he had brushed her off, Carroll had closed her eyes, opened them, and looked at the verse again. That time, the well-known words had appeared: "In the year that King Uzziah died, I saw the Lord...."

Carroll could not let the revised message go. She knew what she had seen, and she knew that the God who used a vision to speak to Isaiah could use a vision to speak to her. And she knew that if she wanted to see God—*really* see him in the close and intimate relationship she wanted—she would have to let her marriage die the death it had already begun.

Resolutely, Carroll slid into the car and closed the door. "Okay, Mom, let's go." And the white Renault left Joshua standing in a cloud of dust.

- -

HRH Princess Carroll Ayo Durodola's resolve later fell prey to her husband's pleadings and promises to reform, and she returned to an off-again/on-again marriage that took years to die. Now living in the United States, she enjoys the deeper relationship with God that he intended when he sent the vision. Through her website at www.princessayo.com, she maintains a ministry of Christian education consulting, writing, art, and storytelling in the African tradition. Her children's book, 'Tunde, the Little Nigerian Prince, tells the story of her father and his youthful commitment to Christ through the persistent efforts of an American missionary in Nigeria.

Headlights

This is the message we have heard from him and declare to you: God is light; in him there is no darkness at all.
1 John 1:5

Two young women were driving a deserted highway alone at night. This was not a good idea, even in the 1980s. But Mary and Jane were identical twins and they didn't have a typical concept of "alone." They were never alone because they always had each other. To them, this was not unusual; it was simply the way they had grown up.

They could have gone to different colleges had they wanted to, but they didn't. They both wanted to attend the University of Kentucky, and as high school seniors, they had already applied for admission. They were thrilled to come home from school one afternoon and greet two fat envelopes from UK.

The teenagers were ecstatic. The envelopes, even before opened, shouted a message every aspiring college applicant knew how to interpret. Thin envelopes were rejections—How much paper does it take to say no?—and fat envelopes were acceptances. The stuffed packets, filled with numerous information sheets and blank forms to be completed and returned to the school, contained everything needed to make their invitation official to become students at the University.

Praise the Lord for fat envelopes.

Now at UK, it was late on Friday afternoon. Classes had dismissed for the weekend and the sisters missed their folks. "Let's run down to Madisonville for the weekend," Mary suggested.

"Good idea," agreed Jane.

Throwing their packed overnight bags into the back seat of their 1979 Mustang, and a few books to present a studious front to their parents, they jumped into the car and hit the road with Mary at the wheel.

From the University, take New Circle Road around the edge of Lexington to the Bluegrass Parkway toward Elizabethtown, then take the West Kentucky Parkway to northbound Pennyrile Parkway and hop off at one of two exits for Madisonville. It wasn't a straight shot, but it was a routine drive and they had made the 190-mile trip many times. They could do it in the dark, and this time, they would. Literally.

The sisters were somewhere west of Elizabethtown when, suddenly and without warning, the Mustang's headlights blacked out. Zap, just like that. The headlights didn't merely dim; they shut completely off.

How far can a car travel at 65 miles per hour before the driver can brake it? Too far. How can the driver pull the car onto the shoulder when the shoulder is invisible? She can't. The Mustang speeding down the road in pitch-blackness and Mary's heart racing, she braked the car and slowed as she quickly realized—Wonder of wonders!—the parking lights were still on. From the small measure of dim light cast low on the road, she could see, if only barely, a very short strip of dark asphalt.

How could the parking lights work when the headlights didn't? Because they were on separate electrical circuits and had separate switches. But neither of the sisters knew that. In fact, they had never even wondered about it. They approached a car the same way they approached other mechanical devices. Things do their jobs when people do theirs; that's the way life works. And why not? An understanding of automotives is no more necessary to the operation of a car than is an understanding of a TV remote device to the operation of the set.

Now Mary and Jane wished they knew something—almost anything—about cars. If the headlights had failed, perhaps something else was about to fail, something that could leave them stranded. They would feel better if they knew why the headlights had gone out, even if they didn't know what to do about it.

What they knew was that the West Kentucky Parkway is a sparsely traveled stretch of road, two lanes on each side with a wide grassy median strip between the eastbound and westbound sections. Towns along the way are few and widely scattered, and drivers can travel for miles without seeing another vehicle on either side of the road.

The other thing the sisters knew was that a car's parking lights provide too little illumination for nighttime driving. What were they to do? Silently praying and inching along at a snail's pace to avoid outrunning the parking lights, Mary and Jane considered their options.

Perhaps they should chance pulling the car off the road. Now that they were moving slowly, the right shoulder was slightly visible. They could ease the car off the road, flag down an approaching driver, and ask for help. But how could they be sure the driver could be trusted? Anyway, it could be hours before another car approached.

Perhaps a state police officer would drive by and notice their plight; a state trooper would be both trustworthy and competent. But the twins had never seen a police patrol car along this stretch of road, so that possibility held little promise.

No, they would proceed slowly and pray that they could make it to the Beaver Dam exit before a westbound driver rammed their Mustang in the rear. For once, it seemed a good thing that so few cars traveled this stretch of road.

"If they hit us from the rear it's their fault," Mary said, laughing in an improvised version of whistling in the dark, not at all certain that the Mustang's taillights were illuminated. The sisters didn't say it, but they both knew they could be just as dead in an accident that was not their fault as one that was.

In what seemed like hours, Mary and Jane saw the sign of the Beaver Dam exit ahead. Rejoicing, Mary pulled off the Parkway and into the rest area. But the sisters' joy turned to despair when they learned that the only attendant on duty knew no more about automobiles than they did. And in a move the twins would later question themselves about, they didn't think to look for a pay telephone. Perhaps there was none. Otherwise, the attendant likely would have suggested that they use it to call for help.

Feeling it would be unsafe to lock themselves in the car at the rest stop and doze until daylight, Mary pulled the slow-moving car back on the road. With about 50 miles to go to reach Madisonville, the young women dreaded to think how long it would take to drive the distance at 10 miles an hour. Don't even do the math; best not to think about it.

Suddenly, Mary caught a glint of light in her rearview mirror. Throwing it a glance, she saw headlights approaching, the lights growing bigger as the car came nearer. "Someone's coming up from behind," said Mary. *Please, God, let the driver see us in time to avoid hitting us.* He did. Slowing to a crawl behind them, the driver lingered and showed no signs of intent to pass.

He knows we're in trouble and he's staying with us, thought Mary, periodically glancing into her rearview mirror in a futile effort to see the face of the driver. In the darkness behind the rear car's windshield, the driver remained invisible. *Or maybe he's going to force us off the road and rape us.* Mary kept her fearful thoughts to herself lest she mention a possibility her sister had not considered. *No, he can see that there are two of us. He probably won't risk trying to take two of us down at once. But maybe he has a friend with him, a man. – Oh, but maybe the driver is a woman. Wouldn't that be nice!*

Suddenly the rear car veered to the center of the road behind them, the left headlight casting enough light in front of the Mustang to illuminate the road ahead. *He's moving around to pass,* thought Mary. But the rear car remained behind and in the center of the road. "Oh, look what he's doing!" cried Mary, instinctively availing herself of the most creative example of emergency lighting she had ever seen. Gradually picking up speed, Mary accelerated, the rear car matching her speed until both cars soon were driving at almost the limit.

For 50 miles, the two cars traveled in this fashion, the front car in the right travel lane and the rear car in the center of the road to light the way for the Mustang. Would the rear car abandon the sisters when they reached the exit for Pennyrile Parkway and turned north toward Madisonville? No, when Mary rolled down her window, stuck her left arm out and bent it at the elbow to signal a right turn, the driver of the rear car turned on his right turn signal to show that he had seen her, and followed.

As soon as the two cars drove into town where streetlamps, pay phones and service stations were plentiful, the rear car dropped back and disappeared, vanishing as quickly as it had appeared. *Thank you, God, for sending the angel.*

An angel? But how did the young women know the driver was an angel? Couldn't he have been a person behaving as an angel? It wasn't an issue for the twins; they knew what they needed to know. Whoever was the driver, God was the sender. Just as God had promised Moses that he would send an angel to guard Moses and the Israelites along the way and guide them to the place God had prepared for them (Exodus 23:20), he had sent an angel-driver to guard Mary and Jane along the way and guide them to the place he prepared for them. Because they follow a God who is light, and in him is no darkness at all.

- -

Mary Allard and her sister, Jane, live in Madisonville, Kentucky. Two more of Mary's experiences with God appear in "Phone" and "Drummer."

Parable

Consider the ravens: They do not sow or reap, they
have no storeroom or barn; yet God feeds them.
And how much more valuable you are than birds!
Luke 12:24

His business was down the drain. Kaput. Not that Navigate, Inc. hadn't done a good job; it had. It was the economy, stupid—and long before the phrase was widely used in Bill Clinton's successful 1992 presidential bid against George H.W. Bush.

US government cutbacks in procurement, intended to reduce expenses, also had cut back income to companies that provided goods and services to the government. Richard's company of some 240 employees designed and built large one-of-a-kind material handling systems for military supply bases that stock or modify aircraft engines and similar equipment. But the government wasn't buying any more computer-controlled cranes and conveyer belt systems—at least, not now.

Richard was down but not out. Caught in the nationwide recession of the 1970s, he was trained and capable, intelligent and resourceful. He could handle this, especially since he had considerable management experience and was highly motivated. And with wife Marge to support, a mortgage on their Florida home, and son John barely out of his teens and still at home, Richard was *very* highly motivated.

Reorganization was Richard's answer. He would make Navigate leaner, if not meaner. He would close some plants, reduce staff, propose smaller material handling systems, and keep going. But the reorganized business didn't work, either; the government simply wasn't buying.

If doing the same thing and expecting a different result is a definition of insanity, no way was Richard insane. Plan A was out; Plan B was in. This time, he would not organize a company and sell its business product. This time, he would organize himself and sell his professional services. Yes, that was the answer; he would take a job with another company.

The classified ads of the newspaper became Richard's new best friend. He spent hours picking through the help-wanted ads circling the jobs he could qualify for and sending out resumes. He made cold calls to businesses where he filled in employment applications and hounded human resource departments for interviews. The best jobs are not advertised, Richard knew. The best jobs are obtained by knowing someone, or by knowing someone who knows someone. He tapped his friends and business acquaintances, working his personal and professional network so hard that he feared people would run in the opposite direction when they saw him coming.

Nothing happened.

Richard and Marge had equity in their house, so they took out a second mortgage. With living expenses covered, Marge shopped sales, cut out newspaper coupons for food and personal care items, and did everything else she knew to reduce family expenses. From outward appearances, nothing in their lifestyle changed. But if living on borrowed money was not a long-term solution, what was? Richard prayed about it regularly.

A year went by. As grateful as he was for what he had, he envied people who went to work every morning. How he longed for that opportunity again! Finally, he took a low-paying job at the county court house, a temporary job created by the government specifically for workers dislocated by the recession. The meager income helped, but again, it was not a long-term solution.

One day, a misdirected bird flew down Marge and Richard's living room chimney. Trapped, the poor frightened creature—a cockatoo-like bird Richard had never before seen locally—fluttered and chirped, bumping into one chimney wall and bouncing to the other in a frantic effort to find its way back up the chimney. Finally, the bird settled on an internal ledge just above the fireplace, alternating brief periods of rest with futile periods of thrashing about and chirping. It was a terrible thing to hear. What could Richard do?

Dragging a ladder out of the garage, Richard and John climbed up on the roof of the house. What they intended to do once they got there they had no idea, but they had to try something. Peering down the chimney, they decided to offer food and water to the bird until they could think of a way to free it.

Back down the ladder they went to collect a ball of twine and fill a cup with fresh water and another cup with bread crumbs. Back up the ladder they went to lower the food and water to the bird. If it couldn't get out of the chimney, at least it wouldn't starve.

Then—brainstorm! Perhaps the bird would climb out if it had something to use as a foothold. Maybe a tiny bird ladder from Lowe's Home Improvement. No? Perhaps a tree branch. Yes! A branch from a nearby bamboo tree would be thin enough and long enough and the small limbs of the branch could serve as ladder rungs.

Richard and John descended the ladder and cut the branch, stripped its arms of leaves, carried the branch up on the roof and poked it down the chimney. The bird didn't budge, except occasionally to renew its futile thrashing about on the ledge inside the chimney. Perhaps the limb looked like a barrier to the bird. *Please, little bird; it will work if you'll try it.*

It didn't, and hours went by. The family gathered in the living room and watched in helplessness. Then Marge had an idea. Perhaps if they covered the chimney to block light coming from above, the bird would see that it could not go out the way it came in. They then could shine a light up the chimney from the hearth. The bird could see that the fireplace was a new way out, fly into the living room, and find the open door to the outside.

Back up the ladder went Richard and John, moving the plywood chimney cover from its storage place on the roof and capping the chimney. Then—success! With no light coming from above, the bird flew toward the only patch of light it could see.

Once in the fireplace, the bird lingered a moment to get its bearing and then flew into the living room. Flitting round and round as the family watched anxiously, the bird soon discovered the open door and escaped to freedom.

There's a message here, thought Richard. *God sent the bird to teach me something.* Almost instantly, it came to him.

The plight of the bird was a parable. Richard had been flapping around like the bird trying this and that, but his way out of joblessness would not be by the way he had come. It would be by a different route. He needed to fly toward the light in a completely new direction. The process would involve several steps and several people, and in the meantime, his family's needs would be met. "You will be restored," God seemed to be saying. "I have showed you that the bird is valuable. Are you not more valuable than he?"

A few days later, the phone rang. "I hear you're looking for a job," said Richard's friend in California. A job was available for someone with experience in government contract administration. It wouldn't use the full range of Richard's experience, but it would use one of his major skill sets.

Richard flew out for an interview and landed the job. Flying back home, he and Marge packed up their household and personal belongings, put their Florida house up for rent, and moved to Los Angeles County. John, by then a college student, stayed behind in Florida.

A few years went by and another opportunity presented itself. Richard became project manager for a company putting together a space guidance system—a job that used his engineering experience in inertial navigation systems.

More years passed and with them came another opportunity. Richard joined another company to set up a new engineering department contracted to design a large material handling system—a job that used Richard's experience in doing just that.

Meanwhile, on the side, Richard and Marge started a small screen printing business to apply corporate names and logos onto shirts, jackets, caps, and other employee apparel. The business required only a small investment up front and no big manufacturing plant or storage warehouse. Richard and Marge purchased their goods and supplies only after orders were in hand, so the risk was minimal. They did the work together, hiring college students for part-time help as needed, and that was fun. They would have a good retirement business until they returned to Florida to live, so they could be as busy or as relaxed as they wanted. But almost better was the part about the income, for the Manatee Screen Printing Company provided more income to the family than had any of Richard's other jobs or businesses.

It took 15 years, but it happened. Richard's career was restored—after he flew toward the light, traveled 2,000 miles in the opposite direction, took distinctly separate steps, and relied on the help of others. It was the way things should be. God had taken care of Richard just as he had taken care of the bird. And just as he had promised.

- -

Richard Parvin retired from the screen printing company in 1992. He and Marge live in Clearwater, Florida, where he is compiling a faith journal as a legacy for his children. Another of Richard's experiences with God is told in "Roadblock."

Question

*In the beginning God created the heavens and the
earth. Now the earth was formless and empty,
darkness was over the surface of the deep, and the
Spirit of God was hovering over the waters. And
God said, "Let there be light," and there was light.*
Genesis 1:1-3

No fill-in-the-blanks. No multiple-choice where a guess
might work. No decision trees of "if-this, then-that." No
second chances and no do-overs; this was it. Ann had to get
it right—not just for herself, but for the children.

She didn't like sunflower seeds. She had tried them and
spit them out every time. Pumpkin seeds yes, sunflower
seeds no. It was not a problem; neither was a staple of life.

Now she needed something to fend off her hunger. The
real estate office she managed had recently merged with
another office, and if she stopped to eat lunch, she would
be late to teach the class for the new agents. Resorting to
the office snack box, she searched for something
moderately healthful. There it was: a sunflower seed energy
bar. It would have an abundance of calories but also some
protein and fiber. It would do.

With the first bite, the inside of Ann's mouth felt
smooth and itchy, as if slathered with a coating of grease.
With the second bite, the smooth itchy feeling grew more
pronounced.

Ann walked down the hall to her husband's office and
presented her open mouth to him—just one advantage of
working together in the same office. "No," Al said, peering
inside. "I don't see anything unusual."

73

How often does anyone outside the medical or dental profession look inside someone else's mouth to know what "unusual" is? Neither Ann nor Al knew it, but the roof of her mouth felt smooth because rapidly swelling tissues had evened out the typical ridges inside.

With the third bite, Ann was convinced something was wrong. On the premise that it was better to be safe than sorry, she spit the food out and phoned Dr. Narayan. Her doctor would know what to do if something were wrong, and if it weren't, Ann would feel better after hearing him say that.

When his receptionist answered Dr. Narayan's phone, Ann told her what had happened. The receptionist put down the phone and consulted the doctor, then returned to the phone. "Dr. Narayan wants you to go to the ER," she said, as routinely as if she said these words a hundred times a day.

Maybe she did, but Ann had never before heard them.

Neither Ann nor Al is the excitable type. Still, as Al maneuvered their car through the afternoon traffic, Ann felt the urgency to get to the emergency room more keenly than he seemed to feel it. "If I am supposed to go to the ER, don't you think we should go a little faster?" she pleaded. The uncertainty awaiting her at the ER loomed and her thoughts turned to their children.

Their six-year-old daughter and three-year-old son meant everything to Ann. She considered them a gift from God, a fulfillment that had wiped out frustrating years of unsuccessful efforts to conceive a child.

The adoptions had not come quickly. Once she and Al had given up hope of having a baby, Ann was willing to adopt a child but Al wasn't sure. Years of indecision dragged by. When an attorney told Ann that a woman did not need her husband's consent to adopt a child, Ann decided to act. She would proceed with the adoption, she told Al—with him, she hoped, but without him if necessary.

Perhaps he was surprised at the news or perhaps he only needed Ann's strong stand as motivation. In any case, Al agreed. "Count me in," he said.

Ann had always been spiritual, but she had let her career take precedence and was not serving God as she had in the past. Determined to get back on track, Ann bargained with God. If he would make it possible for Al and her to adopt a child, she would become more involved in doing God's work at church.

Eagerly she and Al filled in the application forms; not so eagerly they received the responses. "Outside the age range," wrote adoption officials on the forms, or "not of age." Al and Ann were not old by most standards, but officials wanted parents who were young enough to see their adopted children grow to maturity, and would-be parents in their 40s who wanted an infant might not meet that standard.

The couple turned to sources of private adoption, and finally, a committed adoption attorney brought good news. A child would be available a few months later when the mother delivered. But when the time came, the mom changed her mind and refused to give up the baby. Disappointed, Ann struggled to be happy for the child. It was for the best, Ann told herself. If the mother wanted the baby, things were as they should be. Still, Ann nursed the wounds of dashed hope.

That summer on a trip to the state fair, Al won a huge stuffed toy—a girl doll delightfully decked out in a frilly pink dress—and gave the doll to Ann. Carrying it among the booths and amusement rides ringing the fairgrounds, Ann smiled. She knew the doll represented Al's expectation, as well as hers, that someday they would have a little girl to play with the doll.

Soon the much-anticipated phone call came. Their prayers had been answered; a baby would be available in four months. Anne was euphoric and excitedly began marking off the days on the calendar. Then came another phone call. "Would you be interested in a little three-year-old girl?" asked the adoption attorney.

"Yes, oh yes," bubbled Ann. "We've been feeling all along that we were going to get a little girl."

Driving to the attorney's office, Ann and Al switched on the radio and the voice of a female country singer filled the car. She was the happiest girl in the whole USA, she sang joyously. *No, you're not,* thought Ann. *No, you're not—I am!* First the doll and now the song; two good signs.

Thirty days later, Ann and Al brought home their three-year-old daughter. Now, wouldn't it be nice to have a son? Three months later, a two-day-old baby boy came to join the family. Ann relished the joy of caring for her little girl and her long awaited infant son. Ann and Al's prayers had been answered; they finally had the family of their dreams.

At the ER, Ann's thoughts focused on the children while Al made the phone calls necessary to arrange for their care. A nurse gave Ann two injections and handed her one of those nondescript hospital gowns that every patient hates. Does the opening with the little string ties go in front or in back?

Absent instructions, Ann decided on the back. Undressing and donning the shapeless gown, she climbed up on the examination table and dangled her feet off the side, looking about the room at the other patients. Some

were old and some were young. Some showed obvious
discomfort and some showed only a detached resignation.
Some had invisible internal disorders and some had visible
external injuries. But everyone wore a serious look. *Why
am I here? This is silly. Whatever is wrong with me, it's not
that serious!* Waiting her turn, the uncertainty built up and
Ann began to pray. *Our Father who art in heaven,
hallowed be thy name....*

Then she vomited.

Darting Ann a look of alarm, a nurse handed her a pan
and slung the privacy curtain around the table as Ann
continued to retch, violently and uncontrollably.

Silence.

Bathed in an abundance of white light and enveloped in
the downy soft warmth of an indescribable love, Ann heard
a rich baritone voice. "Are you ready?"

The voice was God's, indisputably, and he was offering
her an opportunity. She could come to be with him forever!
Ann longed to linger in the comfort of his presence,
desperately wanted to remain cocooned in the unspeakable
sense of well being that wrapped around her like a blanket.
"Yes," she said instantly—no hesitation, no debate. "My
only regret is the children."

The word "children" barely out of her mouth, from
somewhere floated the distant sound of a woman's voice.
"Look at her chest."

I must not be breathing. Straining to raise her lowered
head, Ann spoke. "I can't breathe," she rasped.

"I'll breathe for you," said a closer, deeper male voice.
Then he placed over her nose and mouth a mask that forced
life-supporting oxygen into her lungs.

Ann looked up and a sea of faces came into focus—Dr.
Narayan, inhalation therapists, nurses, aides—all in

hospital scrubs and all peering down at her intently. "We did it, Ann," said Dr. Narayan, patting her on the shoulder.

"We did what?"

Dr. Narayan supplied the details as he and an aide rolled Ann on a table to the intensive care unit. She had succumbed to anaphylactic shock, the body's severe reaction to an ingested substance it considers an allergen—in this case, sunflower seeds. Her heart had stopped and her lungs and veins had collapsed. Twice she was gone and twice they brought her back. The red speckles on her body were tiny puncture wounds from repeated probes for a vein before they found one near her clavicle sufficiently open to accept the catheters for the intravenous medications that allowed her heart to begin pumping its life-sustaining blood again.

Ann began to chatter happily. Nothing could hold her back—not confusion, not shyness, certainly not doubt—as she recounted her near-death experience. She had been to a place of pure peace and love, a place of white light entirely unimaginable but utterly real, and she eagerly shared this news with family, doctors, and hospital staff. None of it seemed strange or out of context, even as she lay flat on her back as helpless as a newborn. Odd how something so unusual can seem so normal! "Thank you for saving my life," she said.

"It wasn't me," replied Dr. Narayan, smiling modestly. "It was God."

What seemed to Ann the shortest twenty minutes of her life had been four hours. From the moment she threw up until the ER staff wheeled her into the ICU, they had been in crisis mode. The ER looked like a war zone, with wheeled instrument and equipment tables, IV stands, defibrillators, and random pieces of equipment unceremoniously strewn about the area where the ER team had frantically worked to save her life.

Ann's mother, whom Al had summoned to the hospital, reported seeing a white aura around Ann's body. Her mother had seen the white light that Ann herself had seen while she was gone! To Ann, it was unexpected confirmation. If light is on the leading edge of God's world, as the book of Genesis reports, why wouldn't light be on the leading edge of God's heaven?

Today, when the time is right, Ann tells her story to anyone interested, especially people who need encouragement and hope. It is an inspiring story of an all-encompassing peace ahead when God's people pass from this world to the next.

Ann answered the question honestly. Yes, she was ready to go but she would regret leaving her children. The answer that made sense then made even more sense four years later when heart disease and cancer combined to steal Al from Ann and the children. Had Ann gone to be with God at her first opportunity, the children would have been orphaned upon Al's death when they were ages seven and ten.

Ann was spared for the children, yes, but not just for the children. She also was spared to spread the good news that those who die in God's love will rise to live in God's love. And she spreads that news gladly.

- -

Ann Goble lives in Clearwater, Florida. Her children are young adults on their own.

Words

*As for God, his way is perfect; the word of
the Lord is flawless. He is a shield for all
who take refuge in him.*
2 Samuel 22:31

Words. She loved them. Spoken words or written, it didn't matter. Spoken, Nan loved the way they spun off her tongue, singing as they sailed into the air. Written, she loved the way they paraded through a book, softly flourishing a tiny serif or boldly flaunting an even edge, marching across the page like little soldiers. Spoken or written, words were wonderful—the way they worked together, augmenting, enhancing, helping one another along. Words were not like people. Words could be trusted.

Nan had been a poet since childhood. Rhyme wasn't important—pain/gain, hate/mate—such blatancy was a poor excuse for poetry, too little reason for being. Poetry was not about information; it was about inspiration, imagination, insight. Poetry was not about conveying fact; it was about polishing up a facet of fact until the truth gleamed through its luminous shell. For truth, simple or complex, was the heart of poetry.

But not all truth was meant to be told and not all words were meant to be spoken. Nan knew which words these were, too. Exactly which words. These words would ever remain cloistered in the deep recesses of her heart, wrapping themselves around her scars like a coat of armor and protecting the secret they carried. Occasionally, when these words swam up the stream of her consciousness and into the defensive moat she had dug around her awareness,

80

she threw other words at them to keep them at bay. Or she played too hard, or studied too hard, or worked too hard.

When these measures didn't help, the unspeakable words climbed out of the moat and perched on her lips, balancing themselves like an acrobat about to step out onto a high wire. But these words were cowards in an internal world where no safety net exists. These words would never venture out on the perilous underpinning where one slip would send her and her family crashing into the abyss of disaster. These words would never tell what they knew, for these words were secret words.

But these words were not just secret words. These words were *the* secret.

The woman of words was using them now. Nan was certain her husband was doing things he shouldn't be doing with other women. Or if not, he was thinking about it. Everybody knows it is not pride that goes before a fall, it is thought—first comes the thought, then comes the deed. "I saw you looking at that woman and I know what you were thinking," Nan said. "Stop it. It's insulting to me. I won't put up with it."

She said that at the restaurant about the server. At the movie about the usher. At the supermarket about the checker. Wherever they went, Nan believed John was on the make, only one sneaky move away from deceit and one dark night away from infidelity.

Mystified, John tried to reassure Nan. He loved her; he wanted no other woman. Nan was not reassured. John's mystification moved to defensiveness. He wasn't going out with other women, he wasn't eyeing other women, he wasn't even thinking about other women. He was going to work every morning and coming home every night, just as he always had. He was a faithful church-going husband and father of a young daughter and a young son still at home. Where were all these suspicions coming from? Where all these accusations? Where was the woman he married? He wanted that woman back, not this accusatory, haranguing caricature of a stereotypical nag.

They had met after her family moved to Virginia from up north near the Canadian border. The move wasn't exactly forced, but it wasn't exactly chosen, either. It was a necessary and successful effort to find employment for Nan's father after the family business went bankrupt when the big chains moved in.

John had fallen for Nan at the start—her smile, her face, her love of life—everything about her. She was intelligent, beautiful, musical, and a Christian. She had grown up in the church and was willing to attend church with John. He liked that. Her family had been through a rough time and had the rough edges to prove it. But they had survived the crisis of business failure and lost income, and if they had been temporarily derailed by the high speed train of the changing economy, at least they were intact. That was then; this was now.

Now, John and Nan's home was like an armed fortress, except with no arms and no ammunition. Unless words count. And they did, in this household as in no other. Words filled up their home like BBs shot from an air rifle, ricocheting off the walls and bouncing onto the children, the innocent unintended victims of parental warfare. In the presence of the children, Nan accused John of adulterous thoughts about other women. He denied it.

Unhappy is the child forced by family conflict to choose between fighting parents, but the children put on their emotional armor and entered the fray. "No, Daddy's not like that," they argued. "He's not, he's not!"

Separated within the same house, Nan and John went to their pastor for counseling. The pastor knew the family well and was gentle but straightforward. Nan didn't have a problem with John; she had a problem with trust.

Nan and John moved back into the same bedroom together but the family was still unwell. Nan couldn't live with John and she couldn't live without him. She didn't want to hurt the family. She didn't want to hurt herself. She didn't want to hurt the children. But the children were already hurting, and so were John and Nan—and she was desperate. Standing in her living room feeling as sad and hopeless as she had ever felt, she admitted it all to God. "Lord, please help me," she begged aloud.

That night in bed, lying awake in the dark, Nan mentally reviewed her day. *Nothing really changed today,* she thought. Suddenly, from across the room, a glowing golden bronze Christ appeared, Jesus in a posture of prayer—right there against the wall facing her—no words spoken, no sound made. *Lord Jesus,* silently gasped Nan, her hand at her throat—and the vision faded from view. Then came the message to her heart, a message designed especially for a poet in rhyme and perfect 4-3-4-3 meter:

> Prayer and patience,
> Wait for me.
> Obedience,
> Follow me.

Oh, how the word of the Lord is flawless! Nan gently shook her husband's shoulder. "John, wake up," she exclaimed. "Guess what just happened?"

John didn't guess, he listened intently and with great interest. The woman of words was fluent, her description vivid. John didn't seem surprised; he was caring. He wasn't unbelieving; he was attentive. He didn't attempt to change Nan's mind about what she had seen or try to modify her words; he took them all in, reassuring her with his unquestioning acceptance. Then he drew her close and held her until they fell asleep.

The next morning, it was as if a veil had fallen from Nan's eyes. Everything looked cleaner, her spirit as fresh as new fallen snow. Now Nan reviewed the facts.

The fact is that years ago when Nan was a teenager, a trusted family member had forcibly pulled her to his chest and kissed her fully on the mouth, deeply and insistently, the way no one should ever kiss a close relative. She hated his rough beard, his foul breath, his groping hands. Horrified, she pushed him away and fled this crime of crossed boundaries and inhibitions fallen casualty to too much alcohol, this crime of unimaginable consequences. For in that moment, the man who had encouraged her trust and received it—that man had betrayed her. And that man had effectively decimated her ability to trust any man with whom she would ever have an intimate relationship.

The fact is that the girl of words had been speechless. Embarrassed. Ashamed. Now she knew why she had felt uncomfortable around that relative, for years had sensed something wrong, always when he was drinking. Now she knew her senses had been trying to protect her. Now she knew she should have—what? She didn't know. She just knew that she had felt dirty, as if she needed a bath, a hard scrubbing with soap and water to disinfect her body of the unholy offense that had defiled her.

The fact is that from there, it was a small step to denial. To Nan, the unspeakable thing did not happen. Or if it did, it didn't *really* happen. Or if it did, not like *that*. Or if it did, he didn't really mean it. Or if he did, it was her fault—or maybe the alcohol's. Yes, that was it; it was the alcohol's fault, not hers. Confused and haunted by feelings of guilt, Nan's self-esteem plummeted. Like a pottery factory second that looks perfect on the outside but carries hidden damage inside, she was functional but flawed.

The fact is that a young woman molested by a stranger can run home for help, but a young woman molested by a family member cannot. Her home no longer a haven of safety, Nan had gone into survival mode. Never would she ever be alone with this relative again, and never would she ever tell her parents. Never.

The fact is that Nan's plan had worked. She had moved on, skittering across the surface of her life, losing herself in her music and poetry, college and social activities, marriage and mothering. It had worked until her husband began to approach the age of her abuser at the time of the unspeakable. Until the lines in John's full face and the hair on his graying head began to remind her of her abuser. Until she could no longer abide her husband's touch and began to construct phantom women as a barrier to defend herself against the enemy.

Until Jesus came in a glowing vision that shined the light of truth on one crucial fact: She who holds a secret, the secret controls.

The vision of Jesus ever before her, Nan moved her marriage from the war room into the treaty room and from there into the counseling room, where she outed her secret and truth took control of fact: Her abuser's behavior was inexcusable and the responsibility for it was his, not hers. And her husband was not her abuser.

Holding out before her the flawless word of the Lord, "Prayer and patience/Wait for me/Obedience/Follow me," Nan followed Christ down the road of truth to health and healing. And into the arms of her husband.

- -

At the request of the contributor, the names used in this story are fictitious. Two weeks before he died, Nan's abuser asked her to remember the story of the prodigal (Luke 15:11-31). Nan saw this request as cryptic admission of guilt and a statement that he had received God's forgiveness. Her abuser did not ask her forgiveness, but she gave it, as much for herself as for him. Later, she told her mother the secret. After a long moment, her mother embraced her. "I'm glad you told me," she said. "It helps me understand your life." Nan and John, 27 years after Nan's vision, are happily married. "Incest is considered...to be a particularly damaging form of sexual abuse because it is perpetrated by individuals the victim trusts and...pressure to keep silent can be powerful as fear of the family breaking up can be overwhelming...."[7] "Early identification of sexual abuse victims appears to be crucial...As long as disclosure continues to be a problem for young victims, then fear, suffering, and psychological distress will, like the secret, remain with the victim.[8]

Journey

For my yoke is easy and my burden is light.
Matthew 11:30

She didn't consider it a burden, so she gave no thought to whether it was heavy or light. Dede didn't sugarcoat it, though. In no way was it easy.

It started when Angela was nine years old, talkative and generally happy. First came the headaches and then came the vomiting in the mornings when she arose. Dede took her daughter to a doctor. School phobia, theorized the doctor after examining Angie and finding nothing wrong. She would soon settle in at school and the phobia would go away.

"Maybe the doctor is right," said Dede as she and Chuck talked in their California home in 1988. They were a church-going military family and school phobia didn't fit what the parents knew of their daughter. She and Eric, her brother four years older, had grown up moving often because of Chuck's job transfers. The kids were not insecure; they were flexible. Still, Dede gave Angela extra emotional support along with Tylenol for her headaches and Pepto Bismol for her stomach upsets.

Then Angela began to have double vision. This was not school phobia; this was a serious medical problem and both Dede and Chuck knew it. "You're right," said the neurologist who ordered the MRI. "It's medulloblastoma."

It was a scary word and the Watkins family had just entered a scary world. Their education was swift and frightening. Medulloblastoma, rare in adults, is the most common malignant brain tumor in children. Angie's cancer was the size of a golf ball and her symptoms were classic. No time to waste.

Surgeons who operated two days later could remove only 98 percent of the tumor.

Chuck was an Air Force officer in charge of hospital laboratories and Dede was a nurse. They were well informed about disease, doctors, hospitals, insurance companies, and the complexities of the health care system. The next few years would call upon every skill they had and every bit of knowledge. And all of their faith.

Chuck's job required much time away from home. After a few weeks leave for Angie's surgery, he returned to work and his life returned to normal, at least in its routine. Dede's did not. Angie had come out of the hospital a different child and now needed extra care. Right-handed, she had little use of her right hand. Her cognitive functions were slightly impaired and she had trouble maintaining her physical balance. With uncoordinated limbs and frequent falls, there were no ballet lessons, no gymnastics, and no soccer for Angela; no bicycle riding, no rollerblading, and no field hockey.

The course of treatment was eight weeks of radiation therapy followed by 18 months of chemotherapy, plus scores of hours of physical and occupational therapy to regain the gross and fine motor skills she had lost when some of her brain tissue was removed. In a family of two working parents with Chuck on travel duty much of the time, Angie's treatment schedule could not be accommodated. Dede quit her job to become stay-at-home mother, nurse, chauffeur, confidant, and medical appointments coordinator.

The side effects of chemotherapy are well known and no one likes them. Angie's hair fell out. "You have a beautiful head," said Dede one day as she bent to kiss it. "And it's so smooth!" Then she left the room to cry. She never used the word "cancer" with Angie, opting for the term "brain tumor"—perhaps as much because she didn't want to hear the big "C" word as because she didn't want Angie to hear it.

The chemo that started in California ended in Bethesda, Maryland, when the Air Force transferred Chuck to the District of Columbia. It was a wonderful change. Chuck and Dede's families were just across the Potomac River in Virginia, and having them near was a bonus for a transitory military family with a special needs child who was easily nauseated and who was learning to deal with the permanent bald spot the radiation had left on the back of her head.

Angela was miserable in public school. Sometimes when the wind blew her hair out of place and exposed the bald spot she had combed over, other children laughed. Once talkative and outgoing, Angie was now a child of few words. Shy and withdrawn from people and the world, she had difficulty making friends and struggled with her schoolwork. Angie was not the same; never again would she be the same.

Home schooling was the answer for Angie through the fifth grade. Meanwhile, Eric was doing well. He was handsome and athletic, a good student and well adjusted. If he resented the extra time his parents gave to Angie, he never showed it. He loved his little sister and hated to see her suffer.

Another transfer sent the Watkins family to Hampton, Virginia, where Angie went to middle school. She struggled academically, undergoing MRIs every six months and occasional spinal taps to monitor for a recurrence of the cancer. By now, she had settled on a wardrobe of colorful hats to hide her bald spot. Red hats, blue hats, purple hats and green; skullcaps, baseball caps, and newsboy caps to match her jeans. *Cool*, thought adults. *Weird*, thought kids. What sixth-grader wants to wear hats when no one else wears hats, or wants to be in a wheelchair from frequent falls and sprained ankles? Angela felt like an oddball when all she wanted was to be like other kids.

Then Chuck was transferred to Italy and things looked up for Angela. She thrived in the small classes of the Department of Defense School and enjoyed family trips to Naples for her neurological checkups. Eric, now of college age, remained stateside.

Another transfer brought the Watkins family back to the States when Chuck was assigned to Bolling Air Force Base. Living in Waldorf, Maryland, the family joined Trinity Baptist Church and Angie graduated from high school, afterward enjoying a graduation gift of cruising among the Hawaiian Islands with her grandparents.

Then the Air Force transferred Chuck to Sumter, South Carolina. At 18, Angie wanted to be on her own, but when decision time came, she agreed with the family that she was not quite ready. She moved to Sumter with the family, lived at home, and enrolled in a nearby extension of the University of South Carolina. But she had trouble with some of her courses and started coming home early to fall into bed exhausted.

One day, Dede noticed one of Angie's papers. Her handwriting, once neat and tidy after many hours of occupational therapy to learn to write with her left hand, was barely legible. Dede suppressed a gasp. *Oh, dear God! The cancer is back!*

A pediatric neurologist confirmed Dede's horrifying suspicion. Yes, the cancer was back. And not just in one place—in three. The cancer was inoperable, but chemotherapy could extend Angie's life.

Angie, now of legal age, was capable of making her own decision and determined to do so. She had endured all the nausea from chemotherapy that she would ever endure. No more chemo. "What's the point?" she asked.

The doctor gave her six months.

The family had been in Sumter less than a year, and Chuck and Dede thought whatever life Angela had left should be spent near her extended family. The Air Force granted Chuck a humanitarian reassignment and in 1996, the family moved back to Bolling, where they received their requested assignment of a townhouse on the base so Chuck could come home quickly when needed and Eric could visit at will.

How is it possible to hope for healing when illness is progressing? How is it possible to pray for a miracle when disease is advancing? How is it possible to walk a journey of faith when fear is stalking?

Angie deteriorated quickly. When she could no longer walk, she enjoyed outings in her wheelchair. One day, while sitting with her in a mall, Dede prayed up her courage and broached the unmentionable subject. "Your hat is beautiful," said Dede, "and heaven is beautiful, too. You will enjoy it. But all of us will miss you very much."

"Mom," said Angie, turning innocent eyes on Dede. "Am I going to die?"

Dede was astonished. Somehow, Angela had not emotionally absorbed what she had intellectually absorbed the day she decided to refuse the chemo. Or perhaps she only needed some words—any words—to ease her into a difficult conversation. Or maybe she needed to hear someone else affirm the unacceptable so it could become acceptable. "Yes," said her mother, commanding the shock she felt to remain hidden and demanding that her eyes betray no emotion. "But heaven is a beautiful place, a really good place."

Angie began to make peace with what lay ahead of her, and one day she asked another biggie. "Mom, is God angry with me?"

This one was easy. "No," said Dede, "God is not angry with you. No one knows why things like this happen. But it's not because God is angry with you."

When Angie's vision became blurred and she could no longer read, she became frightened. What would it be like to die? She was not afraid of being in heaven, just of the journey to get there. After all, no one has ever gone there and come back with a travelogue or video. Would it be like scaling a mountain, worth it for the view at the top if she survived the climb? Would it be like riding a ski lift, safe but a little unsettling?

An audio tape from Joni Eareckson Tada came to the rescue. Paralyzed from the neck down by a diving accident in 1967, Tada is a paraplegic. She has learned to paint with a brush held between her teeth and she has a powerful Christian testimony. Her voice on the tape offered great hope. People will be able to run, jump, and dance in heaven, said Tada. And God will have jobs for people to do when they get there.

Angie loved these ideas. It had been so long since she had been able to run, jump, and dance that she could barely remember it, but she knew she wanted to do these things again. She liked to do cross stitch needlework, read, and play piano, even with little use of her right hand. Maybe when she got to heaven she could use both hands! Heaven would be a great place; she would be busy and happy there. The journey would be fine.

A relative sent the family free tickets to Disney World and a voucher for free lodging. Angie loved the visit to Disney and loved that people in wheelchairs could advance to the front of the line. No lines for rides at Disney. Who wouldn't love that?

Somewhere along the way, Angie fell in love with Tickle Me Elmo and Dede went to a toy store to purchase him. No luck. Elmo was simply too popular to sit up on a shelf and wait for someone to give him a home.

The church prayer network, the cancer support network, and the armed services network sent out the word. Someone in Florida knew someone in California who knew someone who happened to know a Hollywood celebrity with connections. Angie was ecstatic when Elmo arrived in the mail—her very own snuggly little red guy who giggled delightfully when she pressed his stuffed belly. Such a simple thing and such a wonderful blessing—laughter for a dying teenager.

On March 27, 1997, Angie turned 19 under hospice care. She was not in pain—the only good thing to be said about brain cancer—and she enjoyed the birthday party Trinity Baptist hosted in their fellowship hall. Days later, when her speech became garbled and she lost her vision, she still enjoyed movies and Elmo. "I can still hear," she said, focusing on the positive. For true to her name, Angela was an angel throughout the entire ordeal. She always expressed appreciation for help and she was grateful for even the smallest of things. She never complained, she never whined, and she was never bitter. If ever there was a model for how to die with grace, Angie was it.

She lapsed into a coma that lasted three days. On the evening of April 21, Angie's breathing became labored. A few hours later, with her parents by her side, she drew her last breath. "I think she's up there," said Chuck, looking heavenward.

Such a long journey, so many years and so many miles—miles that spanned the continent and twice spanned the ocean. How could it be over in an instant?

When people can't stand the pressure, their seams pop. Dede and Chuck's seams had not popped during Angie's illness and they did not pop now. Sad but unwavering, they made their painful and customary phone calls to family members, friends, Chuck's co-workers, and their pastor. Finally, the bone-weary parents collapsed into bed.

Emotionally drained, Chuck fell asleep but Dede lay awake, too exhausted to sleep. Scenes of Angie over the past few years flashed across Dede's mind like heat lightening in summertime. Angie picking herself up after a fall. Angie glowing in the thrill of accomplishment. Angie placing her faith in God. Angie blowing out her birthday candles. Angie reaching out to help another child struggling with a disability. Angie adjusting her wig for her high school graduation portrait. Dede took pride in Angie's courage, delighted in the joy of loving her. *She is in a good place,* thought Dede.

Then she heard it. "It was so easy," said a voice— Angie's voice—as clear as birdsong and just as sweet. Slipping through the stillness of night like peace slipping through a ceasefire zone, Angie's voice, no longer garbled by disease, was completely restored to health. *Wow! I just heard her!* thought Dede. *Thank you, God.*

Dede slept.

~ ~ ~

The funeral was over and the out-of-town guests were gone. The medical equipment was shipped back to the supplier, Angie's clothes were donated to charity, and her personal effects were packed away. It was all over.

Except that it wasn't.

Why had God allowed Angie to come back and speak to Dede? But then, why not? Death cannot kill what never dies,[9] said William Penn. But what had Angie meant, "It was so easy"? And what was "it"? English grammar abhors a pronoun without a noun; it makes it impossible to tell what person, place, or thing the pronoun represents.

Perhaps Angie was saying that her journey to heaven was easy. But Angie had known that Dede had not questioned the ease of Angie's journey, and Angie had lost her own concern about it after listening to the Tada tape. Maybe Angie was saying that the journey of the past nine years was easy. It wasn't, of course; it was terribly difficult. Still, there had been times when, like savoring a slice of sugared lemon, the taste of life had been achingly delicious. Times when she trusted that her family would always be there, her mother her closest companion, her father working a demanding job to support the family, her brother watching out for her. Times when she knew that, even if someone laughed at her bald spot, her family never would.

Or perhaps Angie was referring to a different type of journey. Jesus told a story about spirit when he spoke of himself by using a metaphor of a yoke—a crossbar that joins oxen together so they can share the burden they carry. Yoke yourself to me, said Jesus; for my burden is light and my yoke is easy. Jesus didn't deny the reality of the burden; he just said it was light. He didn't deny the difficulty of the yoke; he just said it was easy. From Angie's initial diagnosis until she boarded that long white train, Dede had yoked herself to Angie and helped ease her burden. Perhaps that was what Angie meant.

But what if Angie wasn't talking about a journey at all? What if she was talking about—what? Dede didn't know. Whatever "it" was, she would find out when she reunited with Angie in heaven. For now, that was enough. Dede had walked with Angie, chauffeured her, and pushed her in her wheelchair from earth to heaven. Yes, the journey of pain was difficult, but the yoke of love was easy. It was so easy.

- -

Dede and Chuck Watkins, Fredericksburg, Virginia, live near Eric and his wife, Amy. Eight years after Angie's death, Dede unpacked some of Angie's belongings to give Elmo to Eric's children—twins Kylie and Mackenzie, and baby Adelynn. Now every time one of them presses Elmo's belly and he giggles, Dede knows Angie hears him, too. And laughs.

Edge

*...Now choose life, so that you and your children
may live and that you may love the Lord your
God....*
Deuteronomy 30:19

She felt like a kid waiting to be chosen for the softball team when everybody knew all she ever hit was grounders and all she ever caught was nothing. Her name would be the last one called; she just knew it. But this time, it wasn't a child's game. It was serious grownup business.

"It's urgent," Carole had said, giving her reasons to the woman who answered the phone at the doctor's office.

"Okay, come on in," said the woman. "We'll work you in."

In a city, the office would have been in a professional building, all steel and glass and shiny polished floors. But in 1969, the urban sprawl spreading across the Potomac River from Washington, DC, had not yet reached this small northern Virginia town, and a doctor had to take what was available. What was available was an old two-story white frame house with big rooms, tall narrow windows, and creaky wooden floors.

Carole picked up a magazine from a corner table and leafed through it. She laid it aside. She picked up another magazine; maybe she could find a recipe to use for dinner. Finally, after all the other patients had left, a heavy-set woman carrying a clipboard appeared in the doorway and called Carole's name. Tossing aside the magazine, Carole followed the woman down the hallway and into an exam room.

"I'm Mrs. Martin," said the gray-haired woman. "How are you?" It was a question not meant for an answer and she didn't wait for one. Handing Carole an examination gown, she began her rapid-fire instructions. "Everything off. Put this on. Leave it open down the front. Clothes go on the back of the door. I'll be back in a minute." Then she left and closed the door behind her.

Why do patients in a doctor's office feel so vulnerable? Because they are.

Carole undressed, slid her shoes underneath the only chair in the room, and hung up her clothes. Pulling on the gown, she clutched the front together with one hand as she slid herself up on the examination table. *Lord, please help me,* she prayed, gazing down at her dangling feet.

Knock, knock. The door opened before Carole could respond; just another minor indignity for a patient sparsely dressed and shivering in a physician's office. Mrs. Martin wrapped a blood pressure cuff around Carole's arm, pulled the cuff snug, and—pump, squeeze, pump, squeeze—the cuff tightened.

Mrs. Martin frowned as she watched the gauge. "Are you always this scared when you go to the doctor?" she asked, unwrapping the cuff.

In Carole's fragile emotional state, the nurse's curt words sounded like an accusation. "No, just when I think I'm finally pregnant after 12 years of trying and I'm about to miscarry." Then she burst into tears.

The nurse's cool demeanor warmed as she handed Carole a tissue. "What makes you think so?"

The question was routine; the answer was not. Between sobs, Carole described her symptoms. Queasiness in the morning. Extreme fatigue. Shrinking bra cups. A monthly period that came and never left. She had started to measure her life by the number of days she had been losing blood. It was day 17.

Mrs. Martin nodded and left the room, leaving Carole to dry her tears and think about the woman who had been bleeding for 12 years when she went to see Jesus (Luke 8:43-44). If only she could touch the edge of his cloak, felt the woman, she could be healed. *Twelve years,* thought Carole. *No wonder the woman was desperate! And here I am falling apart at day 17.*

But Carole had a different reason than the biblical woman had. Carole was not concerned about herself; she was concerned about her baby.

Shortly Mrs. Martin reappeared, accompanied by a white-coated, white-haired man with a stethoscope draped around his neck. "I'm Dr. Adams," said the man with the kind eyes as he extended a hand to Carole. "I hear you're a little scared."

"Yes," said Carole. "No wonder my blood pressure is through the roof. I've been scared ever since I figured out what was happening. I haven't even told my husband what I'm thinking."

"Well, let's see how I can help," said Dr. Adams with a small smile.

Carole felt better already.

More questions, more answers. "Okay," he said. "No exam for you today; I don't want to jiggle anything around. We'll just do a pregnancy test. Go home and go to bed for a week. We want to minimize the force of gravity. Call me in three days for the test results." Then, eyes peering at Carole over the top of his glasses, the doctor raised an eyebrow and warned her. "No nothing, I mean, *no nothing.* Your husband has already done his thing. All he gets to do now is wait on you."

Carole smiled, amused at the doctor's choice of words. But she knew exactly what he meant.

That night Carole told her husband. His face mirrored the full range of conflicting emotions she had already experienced: joy and apprehension, happiness and fear, delight and confusion. Finally, they settled down to the job at hand.

Life crawled. Carole took her meals in bed. Read and prayed. Watched TV and prayed. Worked crossword puzzles and prayed. Slept fitfully and prayed. Arose only for trips to the bathroom, each time returning to bed disappointed that the signs of miscarriage were still present. And prayed.

Three days later, heart pounding, Carole phoned Dr. Adams. "Yes, the results are in," he said. "You are pregnant."

"Ah! I knew it!" Day 20.

"Now, listen," continued the doctor. "There's a medication that uses DES to help prevent miscarriages. But I'm an old country doctor and I don't prescribe it. I don't know exactly how it works and I'm afraid of it. You can go to another doctor and get it if you want to, but if you stick with me, it will be just four more days of bed rest. That'll be a week. If you stop bleeding, come back to see me next month. If you don't, get up and go on about your business. And when nature takes its course—and it will, because nature has its way of getting rid of an imperfect fetus—go to the hospital and tell them to call me."

Don't take the drug, don't take it, cautioned a still small voice inside Carole's head. She didn't know what DES was, much less what it could do, but she thought Dr. Adams probably knew more than he could say. He probably had reason not to trust the drug, something he had seen in his practice or learned at a medical conference. What if she took the medicine and it did something to the baby, something horrible? *I might as well not pray if I'm not going to listen,* she thought. "No, if you're afraid to prescribe it, I'm afraid to take it. I'll stick with you," she said, returning the phone to its cradle.

Her husband continued to bring meals to Carole's bed and they continued to pray. After four more days, her condition was unchanged. Day 24. Although it would be years before obstetric ultrasound could routinely identify the sex of unborn babies, she had started to think of her baby as a girl, and Carole was determined to do all she could to protect her. She took three extra days of bed rest. No change. But not once did she reconsider her decision to refuse the drug. Day 27.

The next morning, Carole slid into her Ford Fairlaine convertible and began the commute to her office in the nation's capital. Alone in her car, no radio blasting and no distraction, the ribbon of asphalt unrolled smoothly beneath her wheels as she drove through the Virginia countryside contemplating her situation.

It wasn't right; it just wasn't right. After years of leaving baby showers early so no one would see her cry; after years of choking up every time she opened a greeting card from a friend happily announcing the birth of a baby; after 12 frustrating, disappointing, sad years of infertility— now this. It simply wasn't right! Suddenly, her desperation erupted. One hand gripping the steering wheel, she raised a fist in the air and heard herself say, "God, I'm going to have this baby or die trying!"

Startled by the fierceness of her own voice, Carole slowed the car. Impulsively, she had told God she was willing to die to have this baby. Was she? "Be careful what you say to God," her mother had once told her. "He might take you up on it." Carole mentally examined her heart. Was she willing to die to have this baby? Yes. Her husband would take care of the baby if she died. Still, it wasn't her preference.

Carole eased the car off the road and stopped on the shoulder. Draping her upper body across the steering wheel, she rested her head on her arms and closed her eyes. "God, take me if you take anybody," she said. "But if you give me a healthy baby and let me live, I promise to bring her up in your way." Day 28.

Suddenly, like a low tide gracing the shore, a wave of lightness flowed through Carole's body—knees to thighs to torso and shoulders—suspending her in an ethereal weightlessness. No earthly limitation, no physical constraints, she hovered on the edge of another world, a gravity-free vacuum where everything stopped. Dead. Still. No sound, no need for sound. No motion, no need for motion. Seconds passed, a few short catch-breath seconds. Then, like soap bubbles down a drain, the lightness slipped away. Like the biblical woman whose bleeding stopped when she touched the edge of Jesus' garment, Carole's bleeding had stopped and she knew it. She had chosen life for herself and her child, and she knew what upcoming months would later confirm. She was not carrying an imperfect fetus; she was carrying a perfect baby. *Thank you, God!*

Her husband was excited and her doctor was surprised, but Carole gave them no details. How could she describe the indescribable? Ever so briefly, she had hovered on the edge of another world. On the edge of this other world, she had not spoken in tongues; instead, she had heard a silence so intense that speech would have been sacrilege. On the edge of this other world, she had not seen a vision; instead, she had seen every visible thing more clearly and distinctly than before. On the edge of this other world, she had not felt the fear of the unknown; instead, she had felt the comfort of the presence of God.

Even now, Carole is not sure she describes the experience adequately. What she is sure of is that on the day she hovered on the edge of another world, she touched the invisible boundary between physical and spiritual reality where body and soul are one and Spirit is as real as matter. And the edge of this other world was the edge of Jesus' garment.

- -

God's protection continued to surround Carole Harris Barton a few weeks later when a huge construction truck rear-ended her stopped car at a traffic light in Leesburg, Virginia. The crash transformed her vehicle into an unguided missile that rammed another truck, bounced off, and careened through the intersection before coming to rest on the sidewalk. Carole sustained a severe whiplash injury that put her in a neck brace for weeks but left her unborn baby unscathed. Four months later, Carole uneventfully delivered a healthy baby girl. In the US, an estimated 5-10 million people were exposed to diethylstilbestrol (DES) from 1938 to 1971, including women prescribed DES during pregnancy to prevent miscarriages or premature deliveries, and their children. In 1971, the US Food and Drug Administration advised physicians to stop prescribing DES after it was linked to a rare vaginal cancer in daughters exposed to DES in the womb.[10] Carole is now indulging her love of writing after a career in public service and her daughter is free of disease. Another of Carole's experiences is told in "Tree."

Song

He put a new song in my mouth, a hymn of praise to our God. Many will see and fear and put their trust in the Lord.
Psalm 40:3

The piano did not know Tommy. Tommy's wife, yes, and Ben Morgan, the pianist for the quartet. But Tommy? No. Put a sheet of music in front of him and he could sing it. Or let him hear it once; that would work, too. But play the piano? Not a note.

It was almost time for the other three men to arrive. They would convene in Tommy's living room at seven o'clock, just as always on Monday night. The quartet enjoyed the time they spent together, even though they took their rehearsals seriously and worked hard, each member committed to improving himself as an artist and determined to promote the group as a whole. Their rehearsals sometimes lasted hours, each piece eventually committed to memory and each note dedicated to God.

They were so good that they made it look easy. It wasn't. Balance had to be maintained; no single voice could predominate. Blend was necessary; each voice had to be similar in tone and character. Articulation had to be precise and clean, each word from each mouth starting and stopping at precisely the same time, every time. Dynamics had to be exercised, the *fortes* loud and the *pianos* soft, depending on the emphasis of the lyrics and the texture of the music. Tempo was important, too, the music neither too fast nor too slow. But if error reared its ugly head, it was better to run a song to death than to drag it to death, because nothing could lose an audience quicker than a song

104

winding down like a car running out of gas. And nuance, and styling, and platform presence, and—

So many details to keep in mind at once! So much effort expended to corral each personality and nurture each voice for the benefit of the group! It was worth it, though, because they were doing God's work. From the backwoods of time-honored singing conventions in the barns of Appalachia to the halls of the White House at 1600 Pennsylvania Avenue in the nation's capitol, The Proclaimers periodically left their day jobs to trace the highways and byways of the south and southeast in their bus. Outfitted with sleeping quarters, dining area, and restroom, the special bus allowed the group to be self-sufficient as long as they regularly pumped diesel fuel into the gluttonous 180-gallon tank of their itinerate home on wheels.

Tommy walked into his living room and looked at his watch. Six-thirty, too early for the men. He looked at the piano. He could read music and he knew the basic keyboard—the location of middle C and how to identify the white keys by the first seven letters of the alphabet along with the black keys of the sharps and flats—one set of two keys and one set of three in each octave. Other than the locations of the sustaining foot pedal and the music rack, that was the extent of his knowledge of the piano. He could figure out a chord if he had to; it was a matter of simple analysis. But it didn't come naturally and it didn't come quickly.

For some reason, Tommy sat down at the piano and put his hands on the keys. Then, for some reason, he began to chord some notes. And for some reason, music came—first, the notes to his fingers, as if searching them out, and then the lyrics to his voice, as if favoring his mouth with honey sweet from the comb. What was the origin of this music? Tommy was mystified, completely aware of his actions but functioning on automatic, like a music box after somebody winds it up, each tiny tooth of the spinning brush plucking exactly the right flange at exactly the right time. Were every note ever played and every lyric ever sung floating out there in the universe just waiting for a harmonic convergence to bring them together in the right place at the right time to create a wholly new and entirely original piece of music? Tommy didn't know; he simply played and sang.

As I look into heaven,
And I walk inside the gate
Well, guess who was a-waiting,
For He knew I would not be late.

Hello, Jesus. Hello, Jesus. Hello, Jesus.
For it's so good to be at home.

Then I sat down beside Him
And we talked of things of old
But then He said, "Let's go walking
Upon the streets of gold."

Hello, Jesus. Hello, Jesus. Hello, Jesus.
For it's so good to be at home.

And as we walk through the city
And I look down below
Well, guess who was a-waiting
It was the ones I loved so.

Hello, Mother. Hello, Daddy. Hello, Jesus.
For it's so good to be at home.
I said it's so good to be at home.

© Thomas P. Watley, used by permission

Arriving for rehearsal, Tom Shavers slipped quietly into the room and stared at Tommy in disbelief. Tommy couldn't play piano. How was this happening? And where was this song coming from? Shavers had never before heard this piece. The men looked at each other, both amazed as Tommy continued to play and sing. Their thoughts unspoken, they both knew the same thing. Something unusual was happening, something beyond human comprehension and entirely beyond human control.

"Write the words down, write them down," said Shavers, not mentioning the aura of bright light he saw surrounding Tommy.

"What words?" Tommy asked blankly, unaware of the aura as he stopped the music.

"The ones you were singing; write them down. Don't lose them."

"No, you write them down," said Tommy. And he began to play and sing again, his hands effortlessly gliding across the keyboard as the perfectly synchronized words and music filled the air—"Hello Jesus, Hello."

Scrambling to find a pen and a sheet of notepaper, Shavers captured the lyrics. The music would come later, after the men found some composition paper with its pre-printed sequence of five lines and four spaces, and after Tommy had total recall of the melody. Still later, Tommy would register the copyright.

In 1741, divine inspiration arguably overcame George Frideric Handel, who composed *The Messiah* over the span of a mere 24 days. Overwhelmed by the power of the words of Charles Jennens' libretto that drew largely from biblical texts, Handel is said to have worked night and day on the oratorio, often forgetting to eat. From time to time, as household servants later testified, sobs emanated from behind the closed door of the room where Handel labored over the composition.

In 1978, divine inspiration inarguably overcame Tommy Watley. He does not compare himself to Handel, nor does he compare his short composition to the nearly three-hour-long *Messiah*. Tommy did not spend 24 days composing his piece; he spent minutes, at the most—perhaps two hours, counting the time later spent arranging the music on composition paper. And he did not sob with emotion during the composition, although he did feel himself mysteriously caught up in an altered state of reality. His composition has not been sung on every continent and is not recognized by millions. But his song has blessed hundreds who have heard him sing it at funerals, including those of his grandfather, mother, father, stepfather, and several friends. And many people have requested that he sing the piece at their funeral—a wish he will honor, if and when the time comes.

A dictionary defines divine inspiration as the influence of the supernatural on the mind of human beings. Tommy defines divine inspiration as what happened to him that day in his living room. He does not know why God chose to fill his mouth with music and temporarily endow him with keyboard skills he had never before possessed. But for God's own reason, he put a new song in Tommy's mouth.

And in God's own time, he is using Tommy's song to encourage many to put their trust in the Lord.

Thomas P. Watley is owner and lead singer of The Proclaimers Quartet, a southern gospel music group based in Columbus, Georgia, www.tpq4him.com. Tommy has never again been able to play piano, but his lips still sing God's praises. Another of Tommy's experiences is told in "Play."

Graffiti

*Do not be anxious about anything, but in
everything, by prayer and petition, with
thanksgiving, present your requests to God. And
the peace of God, which transcends all
understanding, will guard your hearts and your
minds in Christ Jesus.*
Philippians 4:6-7

A spring sun in Wisconsin rises like a child on Christmas
morning, all eagerness and anticipation. Warm air invades
the cold and sunbeams paint new leaves with green as
dormant bulbs burst and bathe blossoms with color.

Judy was oblivious to the outdoors; she was indoors
taking care of business. For today was the day. If she had
not awakened with eagerness and anticipation, at least she
had awakened with resolve. Rising early, she and her
husband drove to a Milwaukee hospital to check her mother
in. *Please God*, Judy prayed, *keep Mom safe and give her
peace, and give me strength to handle whatever is the
outcome of this surgery.*

A major heart attack in the early 1980s had signaled
Barbara's heart disease. Two major surgeries and several
other minor procedures followed, accompanied by a
modified diet and medication. These had bought time for
Barbara over the years, but now time was running out.
Doctors recommended another risky surgical procedure as
Barbara's only hope.

Sensing Judy's anxiety, her husband suggested that they
go for a walk outside while Barbara was in surgery. Judy
reluctantly agreed, if only to satisfy Terry. She had always
loved the coming of spring after a winter of snow and ice,

but now the worry that preoccupied her was keeping her from enjoying the soft spring air and God's gift of the changing seasons. *Please God, be with Mom and keep her safe.*

"Look, Judy," Terry said suddenly, pointing toward a trashcan. Bold orange fluorescent letters—graffiti painted on the side of a trashcan—shouted: TRUST JESUS. "Do you see that?" Terry asked. "That's what you need to do."

Judy nodded. Even in her turmoil, she knew Terry was right. This was a message from God. Still, fear plagued her.

As a child, Judy had wished time would fly so Santa would come sooner. Now, she desperately wished time would fly so she could get back to the hospital sooner. But time didn't fly. Walking a bit farther, Judy and Terry approached another trashcan, from its side bold orange florescent letters repeating the same admonition: TRUST JESUS.

This time, Judy smiled. Maybe it really was a message from God. Silently, she thanked him for speaking to her and prayed that he would help her do just what she knew she should do: trust him and dump her worries into the trashcan where they belonged.

As she and Terry turned back toward the hospital along a different route, Judy's confidence waned. Her fears returned, and with them came a surprising, questioning anger. *I am a person of strong faith. Why am I handling this situation so poorly? Why am I struggling with faithless doubts? Christians are not supposed to be anxious about anything. We are supposed to pray and give our concerns up to God. In return, he is supposed to grant us peace beyond our ability to understand. Why can't I trust God? What is wrong with me?*

Then, looking ahead, Judy saw it again. This time, instead of scrawled on a trashcan, the bright orange letters stretched across the sidewalk: TRUST JESUS.

Three times in less than an hour, the same message had appeared at the exact time Judy needed it. Was this a coincidence? Whatever it was, it had her heart racing with excitement. The sun seemed warmer and the day seemed brighter.

Back at the hospital, Judy's mind finally rested. Barbara came safely through the procedure, and that evening, Judy and Terry left her in the care of hospital staff and began their two-hour drive home. But unexpectedly, Judy's fears returned. The farther away from the hospital she traveled, the greater became her fear. More than half way home, she began to cry. Her mother had looked very frail when they left the hospital. What would happen if something went wrong? What if Barbara called for Judy and she wasn't there? What if Barbara felt abandoned?

Just ahead, a large billboard loomed on the edge of a field. And along the lower expanse of the sign stretched the now familiar bright orange letters spelling out the now familiar message: TRUST JESUS.

How could this be? More than an hour's drive from the trashcans and sidewalks of the city, the same scrawled graffiti rose from the grain fields of the countryside. It was too unbelievable *not* to believe. God was speaking to Judy, even if he was using a graffiti artist from days or weeks earlier to do so. Her doubts no longer overriding her faith, Judy dried her tears and acknowledged the truth: Barbara would be all right.

God had wanted Judy to trust him with all her heart and not try to handle everything by herself, and he said so: "Trust in the Lord with all your heart and lean not on your own understanding" (Proverbs 3:5, NIV). But hundreds of years later when she didn't get it, he said so again—this time, on trashcans, sidewalks, and billboards. And this time, she got it.

- -

Judy Sheridan lives in Janesville, Wisconsin, where she occasionally still sees "Trust Jesus" flicker on and off in her mind's eye like the flashing message of a billboard. She accepts this as a reminder of the calming presence of God. Barbara recovered, and at this writing, is in her 80s.

Father

*I will be a Father to you, and you will be my sons
and daughters, says the Lord Almighty.
2 Corinthians 6:18*

A long time ago, she had a father. But one day he went
away and didn't come back. It happened when she was
very young and her mother stayed with her, so it turned out
all right. Now Sally was older and she had another father.
He was a real one, too: her heavenly Father. On occasion,
he even came to visit.

The first time her Father came to visit, it was two years
after the divorce and Sally was almost four. It was Sunday
morning and she stood in her new dress with her mother at
the front of the church in Macon, Georgia, the room full of
people.

The minister, his long black robe draped with a white
satin stole, placed his hand on Sally's head and said a
prayer, then picked up a long-stemmed red carnation and
lightly dipped it into a fount. Holding the wet carnation a
few inches above Sally's head, he gently sprinkled a few
drops of water onto her baby-soft hair. "I baptize you in the
name of the Father, and of the Son, and of the Holy Spirit,"
he said. Then he handed her the flower.

All eyes were on the little girl in the full-skirted white
dress, its sash tied around her waist and knotted in a bow in
back, and her shiny black patent Mary Janes showing off
the lace-ruffled socks her mother had pulled on her feet
before they left home that morning. Sally and her mother
walked back up the aisle toward their pew, Sally leading
the way and both of them smiling. Then Sally did exactly
what she had seen the minister do. She held the carnation

114

overhead and sprinkled her hair with the leftover water droplets remaining on the flower.

If ever there was an endearing moment, this was one, and the response of the congregation was as natural as she was. Adoring her sweetly childish gesture, they beamed warm smiles at her. "Awww," they crooned in unison.

Too innocent to be embarrassed, Sally reveled in those smiles and the sense of love they conveyed. But it was not just the love of the people she felt; it was also the love of her heavenly Father. He was just as present as the people were, and she knew it because of the comforting warmth that enveloped her body.

It was a memorable moment for Sally, but it did not seem an unusual moment. God was everywhere all the time, she had been told, so it seemed natural that he would be with her. Yes, she had a Father, and he truly loved her.

The next time her Father came to visit, Sally was about 10. By then, she and her mother were living in Florida, where Sally rode her bicycle down the street to the dentist's office. In an earlier visit, Dr. Short had found a cavity in one of her molars. Sally was a big girl now; she could go alone to have a tooth filled while her mother was at work.

Relaxing in the reclining swivel chair, Sally gazed absentmindedly at the leafy oleander outside the big picture window facing her. "Open wide," said Dr. Short, approaching her mouth with gloved hands.

Sally opened her mouth and closed her eyes against the fluorescent brightness of the cantilevered lamp Dr. Short swung in front of her face. She trusted the dentist and winced only a bit when he injected her gum with the local anesthetic that he said would keep her free of pain.

Giving the anesthetic a few minutes to take effect, Dr. Short began his work. Sally noticed it immediately. This was a bit more involved than the checkup had been, especially the strange sights and sounds all happening at once. The electric drill buzzed against her tooth, the running water swished in the porcelain bowl beside her chair, and the suction hose gurgled as it drained away the saliva that formed in her open mouth.

Then the pain began.

Perhaps the dose of anesthetic was too small. Perhaps it had insufficient time to work its numbing magic. Perhaps it was in the wrong location in her gum. Whatever went wrong, it went wrong in Sally's mouth. The pain that began as a small ache grew into a gnawing, raw-edged grind deep inside her tooth and jaw.

Oh, no, it wasn't supposed to be like this, was it? What could Sally do? How could she tell Dr. Short she was in pain? She was not a crybaby; she was a big girl. Otherwise, she wouldn't be in the dentist's office without her mother. Summoning an adult-like steely resolve, Sally willed herself not to cry and not to squirm. Dr. Short, noticing no sign of discomfort, continued to work, his instruments whirring and probing inside her mouth.

Sally clinched her eyelids tightly and thought about Jesus. The man who died on the cross was the same as her heavenly Father, her Sunday school teacher had said. Jesus loved her and suffered the crucifixion for her. The crucifixion was a terrible thing, but he had died so that when she died, it would not be an eternal death. If he could take the pain of the cross because of love for her, she could take the pain of the drill.

Sally opened her eyes and suddenly, in front of the picture window, Jesus appeared. From his position on the cross, he looked at Sally with a compassionate face and understanding eyes. What a soothing, comforting look! No, he did not take away Sally's pain; he took away the loneliness and fear that accentuate pain. Her Father was with her, and with the assurance of his love and comfort, she could handle the pain.

Soon Dr. Short put down his instruments. "All done," he said, handing her a cup of water to rinse her mouth.

Sally's pain subsided and Jesus faded into the background, but she would never forget the warm eyes and kind face of the Jesus who showed such compassion. And she would see it again. For the face of the Jesus who appeared to her in the dentist's office was identical to the face of the Jesus who would appear to her decades later in a darkened theater—the face of James Caviezel, the actor who played the role of Jesus in the film, "The Passion of the Christ."

The next time her Father came to visit, Sally was an adult and her marriage was crumbling. She had struggled to make it work, had prayed and done everything else she knew to save it. Despite her efforts, a divorce was on the way, and Sally's emotions ran the gamut of feelings typical of people in that situation: grief for the loss, guilt for the failure, concern for her children, fear of the future.

One day, standing in her bedroom, Sally heard a voice—strong, deep, and commanding. *Oh, it's God!* He had appeared to her before, yes, but he had never before spoken. Unmistakably, it was his voice, coming from behind her and a little above. The reassurance she had sought in prayer had arrived; her heavenly Father was with her and would guide her through the difficult months ahead.

Oddly, though, in what seemed an unfair trick of the mind, when it was over, Sally couldn't remember what God had said. How could that be? If God had spoken, wouldn't his words have emblazoned themselves in her consciousness?

"You will never guess what happened," said Sally to her pastor. Then she told him, admitting that she did not remember what God had said.

It felt like a confession of wrongdoing. First, she had felt sad about the loss of her marriage; now she felt embarrassed about the loss of her memory. Who could hear the voice of God and not remember his words? Many characters in the Bible had heard God speak and they always seemed to remember what he said. Otherwise, the words could not have been recorded in the ancient manuscripts that formed the Bible, could they? What was wrong with Sally?

"Nothing is wrong with you," said her pastor reassuringly. "If God had meant for you to remember, you would remember."

The pastor's words seemed right, and they were. For eventually, Sally came to understand the good of not remembering. Unable to focus on the words, she was free to focus on the message: She was not alone; her heavenly Father loved her and was with her.

The next time her Father came to visit, Sally had publicly accepted God's call to the ministry. Studying at home one night, books scattered on the sofa, papers strewn on the coffee table and littering the floor around her feet, Sally's thoughts turned to God. Why did he call her? She did not question the call itself; of that, she had no doubt.

But why, of all people, had God chosen her? He had a world full of people from whom to choose. Of all the possible candidates, she was one of the most unlikely.

She was divorced. Someone still married to a first spouse would raise fewer cautions in the minds of churches looking for a pastor than would a divorced woman. She was a grandmother. Many people were younger and would have more years to serve than she would. She would have to relocate to attend a theological seminary, a consideration not without its problems. Many people were already located where there was a seminary. What was God thinking?

"Father," she said, "you know I'm willing to move if that's what you want, and to give up whatever you want so I can go to seminary. But are you sure that's what you want? Why me?"

That was when she felt the kiss on her temple—her right temple, to be exact. By now, Sally was not surprised that her heavenly Father would come for a visit. But a kiss? Not that Sally considered any visit from God ordinary, but even by her experience, a kiss was extraordinary. Still, extraordinary or not, it was just what she needed. God loved her. She was doing what he wanted and he would be with her all the way.

Neither then, nor at any time before, did Sally intentionally trigger, or even anticipate, an appearance from God. When he came for a visit, he came of his own free will, in a manner of his own choosing, and at a time of his own preference. It had been that way since her childhood and she had always accepted whatever physical sign he sent of his presence as a natural experience—not a common experience and not frequent, but quite natural.

Why has Sally had multiple physical visits from God when some people who love him have had none? She doesn't know why, but she knows she is grateful. And she knows that when her father went away, she did not lose a father. She gained a Father.

- -

At the request of the contributor, the names used in this story are fictitious. Sally is a ministerial student looking forward to ordination after her schooling is completed.

Star

Then you will call, and the Lord will answer; you will cry for help, and he will say: Here am I.
Isaiah 58:9

She couldn't remember when she believed that thing about the star, if she ever had. She had been a foster child during the Great Depression and she was a realist.

Oh, sure, when chasing fireflies outside on a summer night and an occasional shooting star streaked across the sky, Doris had made a wish the way other children did. But it was because she wanted to play the game, not because she believed in wishes coming true. In fact, she knew they didn't. Otherwise, her mother wouldn't have died.

Doris was only 14 months old when it happened. She didn't remember her mother, but the mother who lived in Doris's imagination was beautiful and kind, dressed in pretty clothes, made sugar cookies for Doris, and loved her—really loved her.

That mother was the exact opposite of the woman Doris's father married when Doris was three. Perhaps Bernice never truly committed herself to mothering her husband's children, or perhaps she simply failed. Whatever the reason, she did nothing to stop the son she brought to the marriage from bullying Doris, her sister two years older, and their two older brothers. When Doris was six, before Bernice bore her husband's second family of three more children, the unwilling stepmother pulled the plug on her inherited family. She kicked Doris and her siblings out.

Who knows how the discussion went in that modest home in Marion, Ohio? Who knows all the considerations, the arguments, the rationalizations? Doris would never

121

know; she only knew what she would learn later. One brother joined the Civilian Conservation Corps and learned a trade by helping to build the nation's public park system. The other brother, fostered by owners of a golf club, worked a menial job at the golf course until he was old enough to move out on his own. And when Bernice sent the girls packing—Doris's sister to live with another family in town and Doris to live with her father's sister in Lima, Ohio—the break-up of the family was complete. Sibling separated from sibling and father separated from children, it was a sad day in Marion.

It was a sad day in Lima, too. Sometimes Doris huddled in the outhouse to escape the family conflict and sometimes she stuffed her face into a pillow at night so the family wouldn't hear her crying. If they heard, they might kick her out and send her to some other place where she knew no one. Doris was a fast learner; she would not take that risk.

The one bright spot in Doris's life was Aggie, the neighbor across the street who often sat in her front porch swing and motioned for Doris to come over. A front porch swing is a perfect place for a lonely child to cuddle with the mother of her dreams. "I like you a lot," Doris said one day when she crawled up into the swing and snuggled down beside Aggie. They both smiled when Aggie put her arm around Doris.

Then one day Aggie broke the news. She was moving to Detroit to live with relatives. But—and here was the good part—Aggie had phoned Doris's father and asked if Doris could go with her, and he said yes!

Doris was happy in Detroit. She loved Aggie's relatives and quickly bonded with Joe, Aggie's grandson. A year older than Doris, Joe reminded her of the brothers she had lost. She and Joe played together and they went to school together. They got into trouble together and they got out of it together. They slept in the same bedroom and they didn't even mind. Neither did the adults, at first.

But by the time Doris was nine and Joe was ten, the adults minded. The kids were too old to share a bedroom, the family said, so they made plans to move to a bigger house. But the expense of moving to make room for a little girl whose father might any day come and take her back seemed unwise. Would Doris's father let them adopt her?

"No," he said, "send her back."

So back Doris went to her father's house. But the stepmother who had kicked Doris out still didn't want her, and two months later, another aunt—this time, the sister of Doris's mother—came to the house and took Doris to live with her in Springfield, Ohio. *Maybe it will be better in Springfield,* thought Doris.

It wasn't. In her aunt's home, Doris led two opposite and parallel lives. At school, she excelled scholastically, made friends readily, and served as high school cheerleader. At home, she slaved like a worker bee for the queen, chafed under her aunt's criticisms, and hated the tension that her aunt and uncle focused on the foster daughter they considered more trouble than she was worth.

At age 16, Doris ran away. But she didn't have enough money to go far and she didn't have enough savvy to hide. Her foster mother soon tracked her down at the YWCA. "Come back with us until you finish high school," said the aunt, seeming more upset that Doris had rejected the family than sad that she was unhappy.

"Okay, but I'll leave as soon as I graduate," she vowed.

Doris counted the days. But by the time she graduated, she didn't know how to count the number of homes where she had lived. If she had left a home and then returned, did that home count once or twice? She didn't know and she didn't care. She was 18 now and she made herself two promises. Never again would she live where she was not wanted, and never, if she ever had children, would she abandon them.

Doris moved back to the YWCA and found a job. Strikingly beautiful and remarkably self-sufficient, she attracted far more male attention than she could comfortably handle. But when Bob began to show an interest in her, she warmed to the attention. He was smart, handsome, and kind, an army veteran and a college student. He had high aspirations for himself and the family he wanted to build, and he respected Doris's vow of chastity until after marriage. Three months after they met, they married.

Doris now had the home she had longed for, one where no one resented her presence and where no one would kick her out. By anyone's measure, it was about time. Prouder of her husband than he was of himself, the young wife beamed when he walked across the stage to receive his degree. And when he landed a good job, both of them were ecstatic. Life was wonderful and they were on their way!

Except that they weren't. Suddenly and without warning, an undetected aneurism exploded in Bob's brain, the silent killer felling him like a tree in the forest. He was only 28.

Doris's six-year run of happiness was over. No more than the psalmist understood why bad things happen to good people (Psalm 73:14-16) did Doris understand, but she did not have the luxury of languishing at the end of her broken dreams. With a six-year-old son, a two-year-old daughter, and a six-month-old son to care for, the young widow reached down inside herself and pulled out every ounce of courage she could summon. Taking out a GI loan based on Bob's military service, she established her little family in a small house in Marion and set about rebuilding her life.

A year and a half later, love found Doris again when Jack, a friend of her late husband, walked into her life. They married, and to their union three more children were born: a son and a set of boy-girl twins. When Jack was sober, life was good. When he was drinking, life was bad. Mostly, life was bad. The couple had been married six years when the alcoholism that ravaged their marriage finally obliterated it.

Doris knew how to rebuild a life; she had done it before. It took her six years. Then, ever hopeful, she gave marriage another try. But the private Tim was a stranger to the public Tim, whose charm had camouflaged a mean streak that emerged in the form of abuse to Doris's children. Of all the things Doris would not tolerate, mistreatment of a child topped the list. The marriage had lasted six years when it ended.

Later, Doris would marvel at the coincidence of the sixes. Six years with her father. Six years with Bob. Six years with Jack. Six years with Tim.

No more sixes. Once widowed and twice divorced, Doris was convinced she wouldn't recognize Mr. Right if he knocked on her front door wearing a white hat and a big "R" emblazoned across his chest. Focused on building a career and caring for her children, she rebuffed every man who showed an interest in her. Of one thing she was certain: Not being married was better than being married to the wrong man.

When the twins graduated from high school and left home, Doris moved to Houston to accept a job in the booming oil industry of the 1970s. Life was good until the oil bust of 1983 took her job. With the local economy in a downward slide, Doris struggled to find employment. No stranger to hard work, she pieced together a livelihood from two low-paying and physically demanding jobs—a day job in a supermarket deli and a night job cleaning houses— before finally settling into a business post in a hospital. Ah, a sit-down job and only an eight-hour workday! It was a wonderful change, especially for a woman edging into her middle years.

Living with different families had exposed Doris to various Christian beliefs and numerous forms of worship. So much religious diversity might have confused a less resilient person, but in Doris, it led to the embrace of a core truth that each church had taught: God is love (I John 4:8). Throughout the pain of lost homes and the grief of lost marriages, she had channeled her heartbreak into hard work and depended on God, the one constant in her life. If the love of people was unreliable, the love of God was not. He does not change the way people do; his love endures forever. Worship in a contemporary church or praise God in a traditional one. Clap hands boisterously or kneel quietly at a padded rail. Sit on a metal folding chair in a storefront church or luxuriate on a cushioned pew underneath a stained glass window. None of it mattered; the thing that mattered was God. Doris nurtured an intimate relationship with him, regularly thanking him for the most inconsequential of life's blessings and talking to him as though he were sitting in the room beside her.

Her faith had not yet encountered its greatest challenge.

On Christmas Eve 1998, the tree lighted for a party, Doris showered, styled her silver hair, and zipped herself into an emerald green velvet party dress. Then came the phone call. While riding his motorcycle in St. Petersburg, Florida, Doris's youngest son had collided with a moving vehicle. Jack, 35-year-old namesake of his father, was hospitalized in critical condition.

Mind spinning like a figure skater at the Olympics, Doris flew to Tampa-St. Pete, mentally prepared for the worst—an illusion she maintained until she arrived at the hospital and learned that the worst was worse than she ever could have imagined. Jack was barely recognizable, his head wrapped in bandages, his face and body battered with cuts, abrasions, and bruises. Both legs, both ankles, and one arm broken, he had sustained permanent and irreversible brain damage.

A broken body is hard to look at, a broken mind even harder.

Doris put on a brave face and struggled to deal with her new reality. Jack would never walk again. He likely would never recognize her again. He could not swallow and for the rest of his life would be fed through a tube attached to a port surgically implanted in his stomach. His speech was irrational and sometimes profane. In full command of his faculties, he would never have spoken to Doris in such a manner.

If there was anything good about Jack's condition, it was that he was oblivious to his mother's grief. Profound and pervasive, the undertow of its eddy threatened to swirl her into a downward spiral of depression. But ever the survivor, Doris clung to the life preserver of her faith and managed to stay afloat.

Weeks passed. Doris had read that long-term patients who have regular visitors tend to receive better care than do patients without regular visitors. She kept vigil at the hospital by day and holed up in a motel by night. Eventually, doctors moved Jack out of the trauma unit into a nursing home that Doris had reason to believe was substandard. Her money eaten up by motel expenses and a job waiting for her in Houston, she began an aggressive effort to move him into a rehabilitation hospital near her home in Texas.

Her valiant effort went down to defeat. Insurance companies, disability programs, lawyers—none of them are motivated by a mother's love. *What if Jack knows me and thinks I have abandoned him?* It was an unthinkable horror. Never would Doris turn her back on her son. Never would the little foster girl-now-senior-citizen abandon her son to people who did not love him.

Quitting her job in Houston, Doris let her apartment go, sold her furniture, and relocated to Florida, moving into an inexpensive unfurnished apartment with only a twin bed someone had donated. Burdened by the prospects of her future, she had no money, no job, no furniture, and no friends.

If tears can be prayers, Doris's were.

Alone in her empty apartment and desperate, she sank to her knees. Never had she prayed so intently, never so insistently. Doris had done all she could and now it was up to God. She would not give in and she would not give up. She would not admit defeat and she would not accept retreat. She would not abandon her son and she would not stop beating on God's door until he showed her he was listening. And she told him so.

Emotionally depleted, Doris arose and walked out onto a screened-in porch flanked by pink hibiscus and facing a small lake that hosted a fountain. With the gentle trickle of flowing water to soothe her weary spirit, she lifted her eyes to heaven and marveled at a celestial riot of twinkling stars. *You made them all, God,* she thought. *Are you there?*

Suddenly, from behind her and above the building streaked a brilliant shooting star. Swoosh—the star, gigantically spectacular, blazed across the sky trailing a wispy tail and leaving an audible swish in its wake.

Am I dreaming? No, I saw it and I heard it. God is listening! Tears of joy streaming down her cheeks, Doris dropped to her knees for the second time that night. *Thank you, God, thank you.* She had cried for help and God had answered. She didn't know what her future held but she didn't need to know. With God's help, everything would be all right.

Sleep drifted in on the wings of peace.

The next day ushered in a chain of events that gradually worked out Doris's faith. One step at a time, she found a job with a firm that provided staff for hospital emergency room services, furnished her apartment, and moved Jack into a nursing home where he was safe and well attended. Was it an idyllic life? No, but it was a good life in which Doris built professional and social relationships around regular visits with her son.

The wish of the beleaguered foster child who had seen great trials did not come true, but the prayer of the triumphant woman who had seen a miraculous sign did. Not because she made a wish on a shooting star, but because God used a shooting star to send her a message: I hear you, I love you, and I will never kick you out.

- -

Doris Vance lives in Clearwater, Florida, where 11 years after the accident, she regularly visits Jack in the nursing home, works with the same firm, and stays in touch with her other children scattered around the world. Doris's father eventually settled in a western state where, at age 65, he suffered a paralyzing stroke. In a remarkable demonstration of family forgiveness, Doris's older siblings moved him into a nursing home near them in Ohio so they could monitor his care. He died never recognizing them but always referred to one of his regular visitors as Doris, the little girl he never forgot.

Chill

Even on my servants, both men and women, I will
pour out my spirit....
Acts 2:18

Maybe it was religious hi-jinks, God's version of a Disney World thrill ride. Maybe it was just a momentary spiritual high, important at the time but with no lasting importance. But shouldn't it be more than that?

It was all because of Norman. "Go ahead, Barbara," he had whispered. "Go on down there."

"But I won't know what to do," she whispered in protest.

"Yes, you will," he argued, gently nudging her elbow. "All you have to do is walk up to someone and offer to pray for them."

She could pray; she knew she could. Of all the things she had learned about herself in the last few months, the most important was that she could pray. Still, Barbara was a little uncertain as she left her pew and made her way down the aisle toward the altar. Maybe she shouldn't go. Maybe she should leave altar duty to the church elders.

She had visited this church several times recently in search of a vague something she wasn't finding at her own church. A few months earlier, she had walked hand in hand with her husband through the valley of the shadow of death. When they emerged, Allen had gone home to be with God and Barbara had gone home alone for the first time in more than 20 years.

They had loved each other since they were teenagers. A study in contrasts, Allen's swarthy skin and dark hair were striking complements to Barbara's fair skin and red hair. They were artfully graceful dancers, and when he led her onto the gymnasium floor at the senior prom, other couples cleared the way to watch in awe as they dipped and swirled around the room like two hummingbird moths circling a clump of phlox in unison. They married shortly afterward and parented the two children later born into the family. Their son and daughter now grown and on their own, Barbara and Allen again were enjoying their couple time together—especially their motorcycle trips with other couples in their cycling club.

In the summer of 1982, the World Fair came to Knoxville, Tennessee. When would the Fair ever again be so close to Barbara and Allen's home in west Kentucky? Probably never, they thought when they heard the Fair calling their names. Wouldn't a motorcycle trip to east Tennessee be great?

Yes, if Allen were feeling well. But he wasn't. Still, he wasn't exactly ill, so when he started to feel better and convinced himself that he would enjoy the trip, they donned their riding gear, Barbara straddled the seat behind him, and they drove the 280 miles with their cycling friends.

It was a mistake. The trip to Knoxville went well, mostly, and they enjoyed the Fair during the few days they were there. But by the time they left, Allen had started to feel bad again, and the trip back home was a frightening ordeal. Waging a constant battle with weakness and nausea, Allen struggled to hold the motorcycle on the road as Barbara silently prayed and the other couples anxiously monitored the caravan to be sure that Allen kept his vehicle upright and rolling. Finally, when they were safely home,

Allen could deny it no longer. Something dreadful was wrong with him.

Within a week, Allen was hospitalized, and within a month, he was gone. From his first uneasiness to the devastating diagnosis of pancreatic cancer and the subsequent period of treatment to his death, Barbara begged God to heal Allen. And when he died, she knew God had done just that. Allen was now where disease could hurt him no more.

Now in her mid-40s, Barbara was rebuilding her life. Wrapping herself in the mantle of God's love, she developed a renewed closeness to him and an undeniable longing for even deeper closeness. The pastor and people at her church had lovingly ministered to Allen and Barbara during his illness, and to Barbara following his death. She had no complaints about them, but something other than Allen was now missing from her life. When Norman invited her to a new church in town, a church with a charismatic emphasis, she accepted the invitation.

The services were less formal than at her church, freer and less structured. The minister always invited people who had a particular prayer need, and people who wanted to experience the Holy Spirit, to come to the altar. Then he invited volunteers to join the people at the altar to pray while others remained in the pews singing and praying. Sometimes people wept, sometimes they shouted, and sometimes they raised their arms toward the ceiling, palms open, swaying their bodies and repeating, "Praise God," and "Yes, Jesus." Sometimes people later said their prayers were answered during this process, or that they experienced a physical or mental healing. Sometimes they said they experienced no change. But always, Barbara felt the presence of God in these free flowing services, and she had come to love the utter abandonment of the order so characteristic of a more prescribed mode of public worship.

Now at the altar, she met the eyes of a woman she had never seen before. Glancing at the nametag on the woman's shoulder, Barbara summoned her confidence and spoke. "Hi, Cindy," she said. "I'm Barbara. May I pray for you?"

"Yes, please."

Facing her, Barbara took Cindy's hands in hers, closed her eyes, and addressed God. "Lord, you are holy, you are powerful, you are loving. Come now to Cindy and meet her need as only you can," Barbara began. Her thoughts completely centered on God, she noticed a small chill creeping up one leg. *My leg is going to sleep*, she thought.

Shifting her weight to the other leg, Barbara lightly shook the chilled one to restore a feeling of normalcy. But the chill persisted. *Someone has opened the door or a window*, she thought. She opened her eyes to confirm her assumption, but the doors and windows were still tightly shut. Puzzled, she closed her eyes again, and in an effort to maintain her focus, placed her forehead against Cindy's. As Barbara continued to pray, the chill crept up her spine to the nape of her neck and then to her forehead, finally overtaking her entire body before gradually ebbing away as she finished praying and opened her eyes.

Barbara looked around. She didn't know what she expected, but she felt so different that she thought she might also look different and others might be noticing that difference. No one was looking at her except Cindy, no one at all. It was an odd moment. Still holding Cindy's hands, Barbara said, "I don't know about you, but I felt something, and I don't know what it was."

"I know what it was," said Cindy. "It was the Holy Spirit. I felt the Holy Spirit come through you and enter my body like a cool chill. God used you to minister to me. Thank you!"

Wow! An outpouring of the Holy Spirit, thought Barbara, delighted.

The next day, Barbara was still pleased with her experience of the prior evening, but she wanted to understand it better. Shouldn't there be more to it, something besides the momentary event? The blessing of Cindy was very real, but for such a profound experience, shouldn't there be something more profound afterward? "Lord, what was the purpose?" Barbara prayed.

The days passed and she kept silently asking the same question—*God, what was the purpose?*—even as she noticed an expanding sense of oneness with him. It was if she herself were more real, her mind clearer, her spirit more at peace. Still, something puzzled her about the experience.

Barbara took her question to her pastor. "Why would God use me as a conduit to touch Cindy as opposed to touching her directly?" she asked.

"You know why," he said with a grin. "God always uses the body of Christ."

Ah, the body of Christ. Yes, that was it. The Bible uses the term for believers (I Corinthians 12:27), and it details many times when God used one of Christ's followers to help someone else.

The answer to Barbara's question had been there all along; it just took her a few days to get it. That evening when the chill of the Holy Spirit passed through her body and into Cindy's, it was not a case of religious hi-jinks, God's version of a Disney World thrill ride. It was not just a momentary spiritual high and not even just a blessing for Cindy. Using Barbara was also God's way of bringing her closer to him.

Chill

God has a thousand ways of pouring out his spirit, but when it works, it takes only one. For Barbara, it was a chill flowing through her body and into the body of another Christian, and it worked. It was a chill with a purpose—a profound purpose. And it was profoundly enough.

- -

Barbara Eichholz is a retired public school teacher and librarian in Madisonville, Kentucky. Today when she hears someone speak of feeling an unexplained chill, she speaks knowingly and with conviction. "Pay attention. It might be God trying to use you."

Odyssey

The Spirit of the Lord is on me, because he has anointed me to preach good news to the poor.
Luke 4:18a

He loved his new digs. His room in his father's high rise condo on Florida's Atlantic coast was a far cry from his loft in an A-frame at his mother's commune on California's Pacific coast. But it wasn't just the digs that were a far cry.

Fred had run away from the hippie life only once. He was 11 and had spent the summer with his father in North Miami. When he returned home to California, his mother's free spirit life style contrasted so sharply with his father's buttoned down life style that Fred was overwhelmed. How could he know who was right? He couldn't. How could he know where he belonged? He couldn't. How could he know who he was? He couldn't. He didn't even know who they were, much less who he was.

He chucked it all. When the officer picked him up, Fred had hitchhiked from Mendocino on California's Pacific coast to Santa Rosa—about 100 miles.

The juvenile detention hall was a nightmare. None of the inmate uniforms fit him and he spent the weekend in his underwear. In *only* his underwear. Fred was mortified. If a pre-teen boy dies of something other than a car crash, it will be embarrassment. No such luck. Fred lived to wait for his mother to come and sign him out.

When she arrived two days later, she was upset. Not only had her son run away from home, but the trip to retrieve him had caused her to miss her planned weekend at Esselyn Institute. A major part of the human potential movement of the 1960s and 1970s, the Institute espoused

137

humanistic alternative education and thought systems outside the current mainstream. A missed weekend at Esselyn was a disappointment and a runaway son was a problem. Who wouldn't be upset?

The repentant boy hung his head. Truly, he was sorry for what he had done. He hadn't intended to cause trouble for his mother; he just didn't like the communal life style. But he liked juvenile hall even less, so back he went to the commune. There he lived on his mother's property in his own separate A-frame house built by a resident 16-year-old boy who had so thoroughly adopted an alternative lifestyle that he made it through the day by nursing a case of beer. In these separate quarters, Fred slept on a horsehair mattress, stoked a wood burning stove, and wore recycled clothing.

Directionless, Fred had dropped out of traditional school in the sixth grade. Now he enrolled in an alternative school where students learned at their own pace. His pace was no pace, and he walked away from that school, too. Taking a job tearing down old houses to salvage lumber for building homes on the commune, he took his meals in the communal living center, a barn with an opening in the roof to emit the smoke of the open bonfire inside. At nighttime, residents intoned Buddhist chants and danced around the bonfire to the beat of a drum as members on the outer perimeter of the circle turned the air thick with the sweet smell of marijuana smoke.

Fred was 12 when a 40-year-old woman propositioned him. No, Mrs. Robinson, no! He rejected her advances, just as he had rejected those of an older teenage girl. Maybe it was just stubbornness, but he refused to follow the path some of his guy friends had taken.

Fred turned to the *I Ching* and its complex Taoist ritual of casting a coin to navigate a series of 64 hexagrams that predict the future. Fred tossed a penny. There was a mountain behind him and a valley in front, read the *I Ching*. Brilliant. But how was Fred to get across the mountain or through the valley?

One night after a communal meal, a visitor stood and spoke to the group about his Christian faith. Fred's only background in formal religion had come from the Catholic priest who sometimes gave him a ride as he hitchhiked Route 1, the scenic highway that traverses the fertile land between the Santa Lucia mountains and the ocean of Big Sur. Except for what the priest had told him, Fred had no knowledge of any formal religion.

The other diners blew off the Christian visitor, but Fred didn't. He took the visitor home with him and poured out his heart. Everything was a mess, Fred told the stranger, especially his life, and he didn't know what to do about it. "Jesus will help you if you receive him," said the stranger, suggesting that Fred kneel to demonstrate his willingness to receive Jesus. Fred knelt and the man placed his hand on the boy's bowed head. "Lord Jesus, come into Fred's heart," prayed the man.

The kneeling boy repeated the man's prayer and felt nothing.

"Just keep praying," counseled the visitor when Fred arose. "If you will, Jesus will come into your heart and give you the advice you need."

Fred didn't know exactly what it meant for Jesus to come into his heart, but he knew that he needed advice. During the next few days, he walked the grounds of the commune and talked to the air, barely noticing the February chill of coastal California where the warm waters of the

Pacific meet the cool air of the mountains and create an impenetrable cloud cover that lasts for weeks without lifting.

Fred began to take account of his life. He was a sixth grade dropout. His work was menial labor tearing down houses. His parents were divorced. He was bait for cougars, predatory older women who probably knew his mother wouldn't notice them preying on her son. "Please, God, reveal yourself to me," Fred cried out. "I need you."

Suddenly, in the 40-degree chill of California's winter maritime climate, a blanket of warmth enveloped Fred, covering him from head to toe. A heightened sense of awareness swept over him and he heard God silently speaking to his spiritual ear. "I am your Father and I love you. If you pray, I will be in your heart and will guide you." The clouds broke and the light of a full moon transformed the sparkling dew on the foot-tall grass to silver. Fred fell to his knees and committed himself to Christ.

When spring came, another unanticipated thing happened. Fred's father flew out to California on a rescue mission and returned to Miami a few days later with a refugee from hippie land.

Fred loved living in Florida with his father and stepmother. What was not to love? He had been chosen! Not only that, he had his own private room on the twenty-first floor of a high rise condo overlooking the intracoastal waterway with an awe-inspiring view of both the sunrise and the sunset from his 60-foot long balcony.

Boundaries for teenagers are reassuring and stability is comforting. Under the reasonable constraints of two caring adults, Fred thrived. Old enough for seventh grade, he tested at third grade level. His father hired private tutors and Fred quickly exceeded grade level. But he was still looking for something.

He found DeMolay, a Masonic organization that teaches young men to become leaders. In this boys' group, Fred hoped he would learn how to become a gentleman. But to attain a certain level of merit, he needed to attend church. "Your mother and I had you christened in the Methodist church," said his father when Fred asked for guidance.

At age 14, Fred went to a nearby United Methodist Church. There, as might be expected in this south Florida haven for retired people, he found 120 people old enough to be his grandparents.

The boy hungry for adult guidance took to the church like a bee to nectar. Whatever the people offered, he wanted. They appointed him usher and they appointed him greeter. They invited him to sing in the choir and they invited him to teach Sunday school. The men taught him to cook and the pastor taught him to play tennis and study the Bible.

But Fred was still missing something. "Come with me to church," said a school friend. Fred did, and the United Pentecostals immersed him—for them, the sprinkling of the United Methodists was not scriptural—and he spoke in tongues. Uncomfortable, Fred felt out of control, as if he were hooked up to a mild charge of electricity. With no context for what was happening and no teaching in the scriptural meaning of glossolalia, the experience was far too emotional for Fred. He abandoned the Pentecostals and returned to the Methodists.

Life was good. It was Bible study and worship on Sunday morning, choir rehearsal in mid-week, special events on weekends, homework every day after school, and the devotional guide of the *Upper Room* before bed every night. Sometimes Fred knelt to pray and sometimes he sang a hymn.

After his devotions one spring night when he was 16, Fred went to bed, fell asleep, and had a dream. He was operating his father's 26-foot fiberglass day cruiser when he pulled into the intracoastal bay and headed toward the dock. Then—Oh, no!—the water was swarming with retirees out for a swim! Quickly powering down the engine, Fred threw the motor into reverse and stopped the vessel's forward progress. The people were safe! Fred's relief only deepened when he awoke and realized it was a dream.

It was almost four in the morning 21 floors up in a 10-by-15-foot room with a wall of sliding glass doors that faced a balcony overlooking the intracoastal waterway. But someone was in the room with him!

Perhaps it was his father, who sometimes opened Fred's door and quietly entered to leave cash on the dresser for Fred to find later. No, it was too early for his father. So—so it must be a burglar!

Dreadfully frightened, Fred lay in the dark pretending to be asleep. If the burglar didn't know he had been discovered, he would take what he wanted and leave. Then Fred heard a deep masculine voice. "Frederick, guide and lead the people," said the voice—an audible voice, not an internal one, as when Fred accepted Christ on the chilly California coast. "Frederick, guide and lead the people."

Fred did not—would not—open his eyes. God was present, too holy, too majestic, too awesome for human eye to see. Fred lay motionless, his eyes closed but his mind fully alert, until the first shimmers of light peeked through the sliding glass doors and infiltrated his eyelids.

The day was alive with sound. The hum of the air conditioning tower on the roof. The roar of the cars on the street below and the dull thump-thump of rubber as tires rolled across cracks separating the sections of concrete that formed the pavement. The rumble of a distant train following the steel rails of the track and the lonely wail of the whistle as the train approached a station. It was now safe for Fred to open his eyes.

Nothing.

Fred showered and went to school, barely able to wait until he could talk to his pastor in private. *He'll tell me I need psychological counseling, I just know it.* He didn't; he advised Fred to share his experience with other students at school. Relieved to be free of the idea of a counselor and lacking a background of adult guidance, Fred was more willing than most teenagers are to follow the advice of authority figures. Quickly he decided. He would tell the boys in his advanced biology lab what happened; he would tell them the next time they met.

"You talk to God and he talks to you?" the boys snickered. "Ha, ha, ha!"

If Fred didn't exactly get it, the boys didn't get it at all. Fred smarted from the derision of his peers, but he knew what he had heard and it was too real for him to deny. He was still pondering the experience when he went to a state Methodist youth retreat where, out of the earshot of other people, Fred told the bishop what had happened.

The bishop laid out a plan. Go to Florida Southern College and get a BA degree, then go to Candler School of Theology at Emory and get a Masters in Theology, then apply for ordination and receive appointment to a church in the Florida Conference.

So God calls and churches send.

When time came for college, Fred's father and stepmother vetoed the bishop's idea of Florida Southern and sent Fred to Emory University in Atlanta, where he became active in the Intervarsity Christian Fellowship and helped lead a campus revival.

But Fred was in a quandary about his call. It would rock the family boat, he feared, if he became a Christian minister in an interfaith family headed by a non-churched father and a Jewish stepmother. Maybe Fred could serve God some other way. He didn't have to be an ordained minister to serve God, did he?

Fred went to Trinity United Methodist Church, where the pastor announced a series of sermons on Luke 4:18: "The Spirit of the Lord is on me because he has anointed me to preach." Fred didn't want to hear it.

He fled to Central Presbyterian, where the pastor announced a week of conference activities focused on Luke 4:18. *It's the Lectionary*, thought Fred— a list of scripture passages appointed for worship on a given day or occasion.

Fred knew what to do; he would go to a Baptist church. Less hierarchical than Methodist and Presbyterian churches, local Baptist churches are autonomous and their ministers often do not follow the Lectionary. But at First Baptist, the pastor arose and announced a series of sermons on Luke 4:18.

Fred gave up. Somehow, when he returned home after graduation, he would find a way to tell his parents that he wanted to go to seminary and study to become a minister.

That summer, the news Fred wanted to share with his folks was like a pebble in his shoe, except that when he removed his shoe the pain didn't go away. One day, his parents sat him down. "We are interested in your graduate school education," said his stepmother. Fred's heart sank.

"We've been talking," she continued as Fred looked at his father and his father looked at the floor. "We think you should go to a seminary."

Whether Fred was more surprised than relieved is hard to say. He saw the truth immediately: The thing he feared had never been a problem. He had fought a demon that didn't exist because he didn't know that, over the years, he had telegraphed his call to the ministry in hundreds of little ways, and his parents had received the message.

What parents can hear their son singing hymns in his room at night, watch him roll out of bed every Sunday morning for church, notice him volunteer for every church leadership role possible, see him active in a student-led campus revival, and not see that he is a young man tailored for the ministry? They didn't have to know about "the call" to know their son. What he wanted for himself was what they wanted for him. Period.

Fred's dreaded announcement preempted by the unbridled support of his family, he was on his way. Seminary led to graduation, then to ordination, then to successive pastoral appointments, each position an opportunity for him to share his faith odyssey as a way of encouraging others to walk their own.

Today, Fred gives a ringing affirmation of his call. A life of preaching the good news is a life more rewarding than any he could have chosen for himself. Because one night on the twenty-first floor of a high rise condo in North Miami, God called with an audible voice. And a boy answered with his life.

- -

Fred Ball earned his BA from Emory University, Atlanta, Georgia, and his Th.M. from Candler Theological Seminary at Emory. He has served several churches in the

Florida Conference of the United Methodist Church, and at this writing is pastor of Memorial United Methodist Church in Lake Placid, Florida. Husband to Kaye and father to Courtney and Josh, Fred stayed close to all three parents, including his mother, who died in 2009 after many years of dedicated service as a Christian street minister in her native Germany.

Tree

The eternal God is your refuge, and underneath are
the everlasting arms.
Deuteronomy 33:27

Life is not a bed of roses unless the thorns count. Everybody knows it, especially single mothers and their children. They may not say it, but they know it. Dealing with reality together and handling whatever comes up together is part of what holds them together—literally and figuratively. "Don't cry, Mommy," murmured Noelle, wrapping her arms around her mother's shoulders and rocking her side to side like a baby.

The 14-year-old and her mother were huddled on the side of Carole's bed that morning. Minutes earlier, the jangling phone had awakened them when Carole had been asleep less than three hours. Her routine of helping to care for George had peaked the day before and she had been up the entire night in the arduous process of re-admitting him to the hospital for what they both knew would be the last time. The lung cancer her friend and professional mentor had fought so valiantly was now exacting its final toll.

"Carole?" The male voice on the other end of the line was not familiar. *It's the hospital—Oh, no! George is gone already!* "I'm your dad's pastor. I'm here with your mother, and I'm sorry to tell you this, but your dad had a heart attack this morning and I'm afraid he's gone."

What? Not George?

It was unthinkable. Death had come not for George, but for Carole's father—the steady father who had never been ill, the rock solid coal miner who for decades had miraculously escaped the dreaded Black Lung disease that

147

plagues the underground workers who supply the fuel for half the electricity in the US. A coal miner who escapes Black Lung can live forever, can't he?

No.

After the walls of the room stopped weaving in and out, Carole found her voice, gathered the details, and gave the pastor a message for her mother, who was too distraught to speak to Carole. Then, after taking a few moments to console each other, Carole and Noelle plunged into a flurry of activity.

George, a single man 20 years Carole's senior, had no family, and Carole was coordinator of an informal group of singles who served as his support group. Noelle pulled her luggage out of the closet and began to gather clothes for the trip to Kentucky while Carole made a few phone calls to line up others to look after George during the few days she would be away. Then she hurried to the hospital.

George put aside his pain long enough to offer his sympathy. "Don't worry about me," he said, managing a weak smile. "I'll wait until you get back." *Wait for what?* They both knew what he meant as they hugged and she walked away silently praying. *Lord, please don't let him die while I'm gone. He will hate that!*

Carole now carried a double load. Her father lay dead and her closest male friend lay dying.

Nostalgia ebbed and flowed between periods of silence and chatter as Carole and Noelle made the long drive across the wintry landscape from northern Virginia to west Kentucky. Two days later, they reached Madisonville, where family and friends gathered at the home of Carole's mother to offer condolences and deposit gifts of food.

The funeral came and went. Functioning on automatic, Carole did what was necessary. She felt little during the few extra days she stayed to help her mother begin a life without her companion of 48 years. In Carole's daily phone calls to George, he always repeated his promise: "Don't worry about me; I'll wait until you get back."

Finally, Carole and Noelle were back in Virginia. Together they unloaded the car and Carole hurried to George's room at the hospital. Nodding silently to a friend sitting in a corner, she approached George's bedside with trepidation. An emaciated George fixed eyes of recognition on her and weakly raised a hand. Then, tilting his head back, he gasped. Gone! In a masterstroke of timing, he indeed had waited until Carole got back.

First her father, now her father figure. It had been only 10 days.

Double grief is doubly grievous. Raging over Carole with the full force of its power, it scattered competing memories of her father and George across the sweep of her mind. Often she felt guilty when thoughts of one crowded out thoughts of the other. Often she wondered whom she was mourning. Her father would have been her anchor when George passed; George would have been her comfort when her father passed. How dare they both leave her at the same time! Carole seemed always to be choking back tears. Sometimes she wondered if she were mad.

If there is no right or wrong way to grieve, how sad is too sad? And how long is too long?

Carole moved woodenly through George's funeral and her obligations—morose Advent, joyless Christmas, bleak New Year's. Dreary February was scant relief from the forced merriment of the winter holidays. Phone calls to her mother were routine and helped neither of them, except to ward off feelings of abandonment. Her friends and pastor offered their sympathy, but they were through with her grief long before she was through with her grieving.

Noelle had loved her grandfather, but they had not been emotionally close; the miles between them had seen to that. His actions had not affected her daily life and his memory was not instrumental to her roots. She said her goodbye and moved on.

Not Carole; she got stuck. She carried her body to work like dead weight and bluffed her way through hoping no one would notice that grief had punched a hole in her heart and let her confidence out like air fizzling from a balloon. Her concentration was poor, her recall of fact slow. Her performance was mechanical, her participation in business discussions laborious. She barely made it through the workdays, dragging herself home at night so exhausted that she plodded through dinner on sheer will power and then collapsed in front of the TV set.

One evening, Carole glanced up and caught a haunted look in Noelle's eyes. Her mother was coming unraveled and the teenager knew it. "Mommy," she pleaded, leaning forward on the sofa, "when will you be all right?"

Oh, God, I'm scaring her! thought Carole. What she had not thought to do for herself she did for Noelle. She consulted the yellow pages and phoned a grief counselor. The weekly counseling sessions at the local hospital helped and Carole began to feel less scattered, but she still felt great pain. One night in bed just before falling to sleep, she moaned in silent desperation. "God, I can't stand this any longer. I mean, I really can't."

How many can't-stand-its does God hear in a day? And what does he do about them? This time, he sent a dream. Carole was a child again, a preschooler standing at the foot of her father's grave. Slowly a green sprig emerged from the grave and began to grow. The sprig grew bigger, rapidly forming a trunk that began to sprout limbs. As trunk and limbs grew, tiny leaves began to unfold, quickly becoming big and flat like huge lily pads. Finally, the top of the tree touched the sky. Then, as can happen only in a dream, little girl Carole magically lay in the arms of the tree, relaxing among the cushiony leaves, peacefully enjoying the sunshine.

Carole awakened, for the first time in months free of emotional pain. Never had normalcy felt so good! Lying alone in the dark, she was as puzzled by the dream as she was comforted. Then a fragment of scripture came to her mind: "Underneath are the everlasting arms."

Arms. Aha! As preschoolers, she and her brother had sometimes crawled into bed with their father while their mother made breakfast. He would draw them close, cradling one child in each arm and telling them stories until their mother called them to the table. "Once upon a time...." he always began. During her dark period of grief, Carole had often reached up on the shelf of her mind and pulled down that cherished memory—not of the long forgotten childhood stories, but of those special times and the strong arms that had held her close and made her feel loved, safe, and secure.

A psychologist may have an explanation for what happened to Carole. So does she. Like Jacob who had a dream in which angels walked up and down a stairway between earth and heaven (Genesis 28:12-16), she understood the dream when she awoke. The God who knew her grief as surely as he knew her life had used a symbolic dream to recreate the comforting arms of her father. In allowing her to relive that treasured childhood experience,

God relieved her grief and demonstrated that he is her dwelling place. And underneath are the everlasting arms.

- -

Carole Harris Barton later married again and is now retired from a career in public service. She lives in Virginia and Florida, where she indulges her love of writing. Noelle is now on her own. Another of Carole's stories is told in "Edge."

Sneak

*Woe to those who go to great depths to hide their
plans from the Lord, who do their work in darkness
and think, "Who sees us? Who will know?"*
Isaiah 29:15

I'*m a sneak and I hate it,* thought Nancy. *But what
Mother doesn't know won't hurt her. After all, it's for her
own good.*

So if it was for Jean's own good, why was Nancy
sneaking? Because she had already tried the direct
approach and failed. Now she was working in the dark, not
because she was hiding from the Lord, but because she was
hiding from her mother.

Jean was 91 years old. She had earned the right to do as
she pleased, and she pleased to live in her own house and
not be a bother to her daughter. Jean and Nancy had just
returned to Jean's house in Belle, West Virginia, after
Jean's extended visit to Nancy and John's home in
Spotsylvania, Virginia, where Jean had a beautifully
decorated guest room with her own private bath. But as
much as she liked to visit her daughter and son-in-law,
there was no place like home.

In the 1950s, pop songstress Rosemary Clooney stayed
on the charts for 18 weeks with her rendition of "This Ole
House." Had she recorded the song in 2008 instead of
1954, she could have dedicated it to Jean and her house, for
both had seen livelier days.

The pacemaker that regulated Jean's heart rate had
eased her congestive heart failure, but eyeglasses and two
eye surgeries had not improved her vision. Until five years
ago, she still backed her car out of the garage without

scraping the fender—Some people weren't that good *before* they were 86—and drove herself around town. Now, however, her limited vision prevented her from driving, and she relied on friends to chauffeur her wherever she needed to go.

As for this old house, its foundation was sound. With its wide front door and deep front porch, the two-story house proudly wore the white aluminum siding that years ago had covered the old asbestos shingles popular in post-World War II America. The interior, however, looked a little worse from the wear—not dingy, just a little tired. Sometimes Jean wished aloud that she could redecorate— spruce up the walls with a fresh coat of paint and maybe hang new curtains. But every time Nancy offered to help make plans for the redecorating, Jean changed her mind. "It's not that bad," she always said.

This old house had been almost new when Jean and Jim had moved in shortly after their marriage. With all the comforts of home, it was the center of family activity when they weren't involved with their other work: Jim's service station, where he filled drivers' gas tanks and passed the time of day, and Jean's dance studio, where she taught children and teenagers to balance *en pointe* or tap their way onto the local stage.

In this old house, Jean had sewed the costumes for student dance recitals and warmly greeted the mothers who brought children for their fittings. In this old house, Jean had sewed Nancy's wedding gown and hand-rolled untold yards of white silk illusion that formed the hem of the veil Nancy wore on the day she married John. In this old house, Jean had devotedly cared for Jim for eight years until his advancing Alzheimer's disease forced her to admit him to a long-term care facility, where he would later die. In this old house, Jean had learned to live alone for the first time ever. For at age 19, like many women of her generation, she had moved out of her parents' house on her wedding day and moved directly in with her husband. And in this old house, Jean was not about to change anything that didn't have to be changed.

If change was out, adaptation was in. Sometime ago, out of respect for Jean's creaky knees, Nancy had convinced her mother to relocate her bedroom from the second floor to the first so she could avoid the stairs. It was easy to center Jean's life on one level; they simply moved the table aside and pulled out the sofa bed in the dining room. To spare her the five-step trip across the front porch to the mailbox, the letter carrier kindly agreed to slip Jean's mail inside the screen door. For regular help there was a paid caregiver, and for emergency help, Jean wore the Alert USA personal emergency response necklace that Nancy bought. For a mere press of the magic button on the necklace, Naomi, the neighbor on call, would rush to Jean's aid. Good, all was set.

Nancy and Jean were very close. They seldom had conflict and they never argued. Oh, occasionally there was a little tension, especially when Jean donned her Mommy hat and casually mentioned—keeping her daughter's health in mind, of course—that perhaps Nancy should eat a little less so she would weigh a little less. "I'm doing just fine, Mom, thank you," Nancy would say with a smile, a little edginess sometimes creeping into her voice. And never was there a fight.

But that was before the smoke detector.

How could a smoke detector cause a fight? Because Nancy wanted Jean to have a new one and Jean wanted to keep the old one. To Jean, it didn't matter that Nancy had chosen the Alert USA necklace over other brands because a smoke detector was a part of the package. And not just any smoke detector, but a special one that automatically notified the fire department when smoke triggered the alarm.

Jean would have nothing to do with it. Absolutely and unequivocally, the new smoke detector was not going up in this old house! It was Jean's house and it was her decision. Her old smoke detector still worked and it was not coming down. And if two smoke detectors went off at once, they would make too much noise. She had her emergency response necklace and she could summon help any time she needed it, thank you. No, Nancy, do *not* take the old smoke detector down and do *not* put up the fancy new one. Just back off, said Jean—not exactly in those words, but exactly in that meaning. And she didn't smile when she said it.

The more Nancy protested the more Jean resisted. Her eyes might not be as good as they once were, but her ears were as good as ever and she didn't like what she was hearing. Neither did Nancy. Their voices rose and they faced off like Mohammed Ali and Joe Frazier at Madison Square Garden. And just like Ali and Frazier, it was Nancy and Jean's fight of the century.

When it was over, Nancy did just as her mother asked. Like a chastised dog slinking upstairs with its tail between it legs, Nancy backed off while Alpha Jean stayed downstairs protecting her territory. When Nancy stashed the smoke detector in a closet and went to bed, the floor between them was a perfect symbol of the emotional barrier between them. And the next day when Nancy drove back to Virginia, her eyes were red. Of course, it might have been because of the sleepless night instead of the tears.

Sneak

Back in Virginia, Nancy plastered on a bright smile and went through the motions of business as usual. But there was no such thing, because Nancy's mind was plagued with one burning question. What if this old house caught fire and smoke overcame Jean before she could push her emergency button? Smoke inhalation can be as serious a problem as the flames that cause the smoke. Or what if Jean pushed her emergency button and help didn't arrive soon enough? Jean could barely see and she didn't move swiftly anymore. What if she fell while trying to escape and got trapped inside?

These thoughts were too terrible to fathom.

Nancy fretted and prayed. She lost sleep and prayed. She vented to John until his patience wore thin. Yes, Jean *did* need the new smoke detector. But if she wouldn't let Nancy install it, what could John do? Not get between mother and daughter, that's what.

This did nothing to relieve Nancy's guilt. She felt guilty that she had left her mother alone, even though Nancy knew it was what Jean wanted. She felt guilty that she had fought with her mother, even though she was only trying to assure Jean's safety. *If only I had said*—Nancy thought, repeatedly reconstructing the conversation she felt she should have had with Jean that would have produced a favorable result. *If only*—

If only it were that simple.

Every night before Nancy closed her eyes, she said a prayer for Jean's safety. And every night after she closed her eyes, the same image popped into her mind: the bright new smoke detector on the ceiling of this old house. "What can I do, Lord?" she asked.

Then one day, she got it. God had been showing her an image of the new smoke detector on the ceiling all along, but she hadn't seen it as God showing her the answer. Now she did. But God doesn't install smoke detectors, so what could she do? Be God's hands? Yes. What Nancy saw in her mind she soon would see on the ceiling of this old house. All she had to do was wait until Jean was asleep.

It was mid-February when Nancy threw her packed overnight bag into her new silver gray Mary Kay Pontiac and drove to West Virginia. That evening after bedtime, in the silence of this old house, Nancy crept out of bed. Sneaking around like a teenager coming home after curfew, Nancy unboxed the new smoke detector, gathered her tools and a stepladder, and went to work. *Lord, please don't let the ladder squeak and please don't let Mother wake up,* silently prayed Nancy.

God was on duty. The ladder didn't squeak and Jean didn't wake up.

The next morning Jean noticed nothing. Not that Nancy was grateful for Jean's poor vision, but just this once, perhaps something good could come to Jean because of it. Her mother none the wiser, Nancy kissed her on the cheek, slid into her car, and drove back to Virginia in her allotted six hours. *What she doesn't know won't hurt her.*

But a daughter brought up by Jean Smithers does not wear deception well, and with the passing of days, Nancy grew uncomfortable. Like a parent preparing for *the* talk with a child, Nancy prepared for *the* talk with her mother. Finally, her courage gathered and her throat cleared one last time, Nancy phoned Jean and confessed.

It was the quietest explosion Nancy never heard. "Oh, you did?" said Jean. "Okay."

Okay? Nancy couldn't believe her ears. *What do you mean, okay? You mean after all I've been through, it's okay?* Happy to be rid of the conflict, Nancy quickly recouped and changed the subject. Perhaps Jean voiced no objection because she had changed her mind. Perhaps she merely accepted that what was done was done; Nancy had seen her mother take that approach when faced with accepting the unacceptable. Or perhaps one of those infamous senior moments had galloped across Jean's brain on a lost synapse and banished her initial objection from memory. Whatever had happened, it was good.

On the evening of April 6, 2008, around nine o'clock, Nancy answered the phone in Virginia. "Hi, Nancy," said Naomi. Nancy recognized the voice immediately and her heart skipped a beat. It was bad news; had to be.

Well, yes and no. It was bad news/good news. Jean wasn't ill or injured, but she was next door being checked out by the rescue squad after the fire.

"Fire?" cried Nancy. "What fire?"

Details were still coming in, said Naomi, but Jean's kitchen had caught fire. Right now, the main thing to know was that Jean appeared to be none the worse from the experience and this old house was still standing. But the possibility of smoke inhalation in a person with congestive heart failure is not to be taken lightly, so the EMTs who responded to the call were insisting on taking Jean to the hospital. As soon as the hospital did their thing and released her, Jean's next-door neighbor would take her home with him, and Mark would look after Jean until Nancy could get there.

Nancy phoned the hospital but staff had taken Jean for a test, so Nancy left a message for her mother with an aide. The next morning when Nancy and John arrived in West

Virginia and found Jean at Mark's house, they got the full story. Jean had been making a late night snack when the electric toaster, plugged into an outlet on the kitchen range, caught fire and melted down. The smoke detector screaming, Jean had frantically flailed a dishtowel at the flames in an effort to smother them. But when they flicked up the side of the refrigerator and spread toward the ceiling, Jean knew she was in trouble. *Lord, help!* Clutching her personal emergency response necklace, she pushed the button.

Naomi received the call and immediately phoned Mark, who rushed next door and led Jean to safety just as the firefighters arrived in all their protective regalia. Like the angel entering the fiery furnace (Daniel 3:28), the firefighters entered this old house as it helplessly watched thick black smoke deposit a thin film of grime on furnishings, walls, and floors. And to Jean, the firefighters were as welcome as the angel was to Daniel's three rescued servants of God.

Sometimes you get down on your knees to call on God and sometimes you get up on a stepladder, thought Nancy. But she didn't say it. And the next day when Nancy and John began working with the insurance company to restore this old house, Nancy didn't say the other thing she was thinking, either. *I'm a sneak and I'm proud of it.*

- -

Nancy Smithers Bowles decided against checking with Alert USA to learn whether the company's first alert came from the new smoke detector or from Jean's emergency response necklace. By the time Nancy thought to ask, it seemed not to matter. Several months later, Jean Smithers left this old house for the last time in favor of a mansion in the heavenly city of gold. Until the day she passed, she rejoiced that her insurance company had not merely replaced her old appliances with new ones, but had repainted her smoke-damaged walls and installed all new window and floor coverings. Now restored to a condition better than before the fire, this old house proudly shows off her brand new clothes as she awaits her brand new family.

Dragonfly

For God does speak—now one way, now another—
... In a dream, in a vision of the night....
Job 33:14-15

The first time the dragonfly came, Kimberly had made a mistake. She was sorry for her mistake and asked God's forgiveness, but she wasn't sure forgiveness had come. Weighed down by guilt and feeling terribly alone, she had fallen asleep and had begun to dream.

She saw herself in her backyard when a bee approached—a red and black striped bee. Buzzing all around her, oblivious to the palm fronds and orange trees, the bee tried to attack, its nasty stinger sharp and its vicious intentions clear. Kimberly ran toward the sliding glass door on the patio; she would die if she could not get inside the house. But the bee came between her and the door, blocking her route to safety. Terrified, she circled back into the yard, the bee aggressively chasing her. She made another run for the house, but the bee again flew between her and the door. Tripping on the edge of the patio, Kimberly fell. Flat on the ground, this was the end. Now she would die.

Suddenly, from out of nowhere, a gleaming golden dragonfly appeared. Flying between the bee and Kimberly, the dragonfly took the sting of the bee, which fell dead. But the dragonfly fell dead, too. It died so she could live! Then, as Kimberly watched in grateful wonder, the dragonfly began to stir. Slowly it rose, gathering strength as it flew into the air. Hovering in front of her face, its elongated body and wide-stretched wings formed the shape of a cross. Then it flew away.

Awaking, Kimberly's rational mind took over. Only in a dream is a bee red and black. Dream interpreters ascribe the color red to danger and the color black to evil. Artists often use golden yellow as the color of the sun, a homonym for son—or Son—and the Bible uses the image of a prowling wild animal to describe the devil (I Peter 5:8).

Then Kimberly's spiritual mind took over. The bee represented Satan trying to overtake her. The dragonfly, a creature born of water, represented the Son of God protecting her by dying on the cross for her sin, then rising to live again in a promise of eternal life. She was not beyond hope and she was not alone. And God had sent the dream to tell her so.

After the dream, Kimberly began to notice dragonflies. Not that they showed up everywhere she went, but occasionally she would see one of the beneficial creatures going about its business of ridding the world of flies and mosquitoes. Every time a dragonfly appeared Kimberly remembered that God was present. The dragonfly became a pact between her and God, a secret between friends. When she wasn't wearing a cross pin or necklace as an outward expression of her faith, she wore a dragonfly—her reminder that God was always with her.

The second time the dragonfly came was the second time she went to the imaging unit at Orlando Regional Medical Center. Her obstetrician had expressed concern about her pregnancy with the twins and had sent her for a second ultrasound. She hadn't wanted to be alone then, either. But her husband couldn't go with her, and her pregnancy was so new that she had not yet told anyone else about it. So she went alone for the sonogram.

Pray continually (I Thessalonians 5:17, NIV), said the apostle Paul, and Kimberly did. She prayed in the car while driving there, in the reception room while waiting, in the exam room while the imaging instrument slid across her gel-coated belly. Yes, she prayed and did not stop. Never had she felt so alone, never so abandoned, never so needy for God.

She didn't expect the radiologist to give her good news and he didn't. One of the babies was smaller than in the earlier sonogram. The pregnancy was not viable; Kimberly would be unable to carry the twins to term.

She looked across the desk at the doctor. He could do nothing. She looked down at her hands. She could do nothing. She felt—what? Nothing. She was numb, helpless, vulnerable. Her feelings tumbling wildly amid her fragmented thoughts, she queried the doctor.

Were the babies identical? Yes.

Were they boys or girls? Don't know, can't tell.

When will it happen? Don't know exactly, but soon; stay in touch with your obstetrician.

Kimberly had one child, a lively, intelligent, beautiful little girl. As much as she loved her daughter, that love could not take the edge off Kimberly's awareness that she would never hold her twins in her arms, never cuddle them to her breast, never teach them to hold a sippy cup, never—

If only she were not alone! If only God would send her a sign of his presence!

She left the imaging center and walked across the street to the parking garage. The soft air stirred but she didn't feel it. The city traffic roared but she didn't hear it. The hot sun gleamed but she didn't notice it. Where was God?

She took the stairs to the second floor where she had left her MR-2 Toyota. What would an expectant mother of twins do with a two-seated sports car? Nothing. She would give it up faster than it could zip from zero to 60 if she could just have the twins. She never drove it, anyway, except when she was traveling solo.

Walking toward the car, she noticed a man about 30 feet ahead carrying a bouquet of string-tied helium-filled Mylar balloons. One of the balloons had escaped his grasp and hovered near the ceiling. Grabbing the string, Kimberly towed the balloon to the man, who apparently had not noticed its absence. Only when she handed it to him did she notice its shape. A beautiful dragonfly!

Taking the balloon, the man's gaze seemed to penetrate her soul. "Thank you," he said, his intensity palpable. "Thanks for rescuing it. It's my favorite one."

Mine, too! Thank you God! You are here; I am not alone.

A few days later, knowing that her body was like a ticking time bomb but trying to keep life as normal as possible, she honored her commitment to work at a charity fundraiser. She was staffing an exhibit when a mild cramp started in her pelvis and began to intensify. *Not now, not now, I'm not ready.*

She would never be ready, but that had nothing to do with what was about to happen. Leaving her exhibit table, her pain more emotional than physical, she now sat doubled over, alone again—dreadfully alone in a dreadfully small stall in a dreadfully impersonal women's room of a dreadfully inhospitable public building. *Remember the dragonfly.*

Horrific moments followed, nature's impersonal violence secluded behind a locked door as a bright crimson flow streamed into a white porcelain bowl and stained its water a hateful red. *My babies, my babies. O God, my babies!* Finally, the cadence of silent bleeding death wound down.

Stillness.

So appallingly simple and so unbelievably effortless was the event that a sense of unreality shrieked at Kimberly to disbelieve what she knew was true. *It didn't happen; yes, it did. It can't be true; yes, it is.* She couldn't still the voices wrangling inside her head, and when an explosive burst of churning water washed all physical evidence of Kimberly's failed pregnancy into oblivion, no one was there to hold her hand, soothe her feelings, comfort her spirit. *Remember the dragonfly.*

After what seemed like hours, Kimberly collected herself, dried her tears, and walked out of the restroom as though nothing had happened. It was a lie. Something awful had happened. She had gone into the restroom a whole person and had come out an incomplete person. She had lost a part of herself and could never get it back, a precious treasure flushed down the drain. *Remember the dragonfly.*

Shouldn't she conduct a small service of some sort? Shouldn't she construct a memorial, perhaps leave a vase of flowers, like the impromptu displays people sometimes leave alongside a road to mark the site of a fatal vehicle accident? Shouldn't she do something to call the world's attention to this terrible loss, to show her regret for the promise unfulfilled, her respect for the lives that never were?

No; there are no social constructs to acknowledge a miscarriage, no cultural traditions to memorialize what might have been, no prescribed rituals to assuage the grief of a woman who has experienced a spontaneous, unplanned, unwanted abortion. The world would never know what she would never forget. *Remember the dragonfly.*

She did, the memory seeing her through the pain of her loss. And today, she remembers it still—to the tune of "Amazing Grace."

> O dragonfly, your arms outstretched,
> You hover from above.
> O dragonfly, you are to me
> The cross that speaks God's love.

- -

Kimberly Leamon lives near Orlando, Florida, where she praises God for dragonflies and her two daughters, one of whom was born after the events described in this story.

Fleece

*Gideon said to God..."Look, I will place a wool
fleece on the threshing floor. If there is dew only on
the fleece and all the ground is dry, then I will know
that you will save Israel by my hand, as you said."
And that is what happened....*
Judges 6:36-38a

He had no intention of working the graveyard shift, not
now, not ever. Just forget it; it would not happen. Never.

The third shift—eleven at night to seven o'clock the
next morning—may be called the graveyard because
nobody is awake at that hour except ghosts. Or perhaps
because many people who work graveyard don't adjust
well to sleeping in the daytime and feel that they're on a
fast track to the real graveyard. Nope, no graveyard for
Fred.

It was almost 50 years ago and Fred was working the
second shift—three in the afternoon to eleven o'clock at
night—at the General Motors factory in Dayton, Ohio. It
provided a good life for Irene, the kids, and him. They had
a roof over their heads, food on the table, clothes on their
backs, and enough money for an occasional movie. It
wasn't the Ritz but it wasn't the pits, either, especially
since the second shift gave Fred the excuse he needed not
to attend evening church services with Irene and the kids.
Lord knows, he had received enough invitations from them
and Elizabeth.

Fred didn't like Elizabeth; she irritated him. She was an
intrusion, always coming to the house talking about the
Bible and praying with Irene. Elizabeth knew a part of his
wife that Fred didn't know and he resented it. "That woman

168

with her religious nonsense is a pretentious put-on. I wish she'd find somebody else to pester," Fred complained. "Why can't she leave us alone?"

And that was only what he was willing to admit to saying about Elizabeth.

But Irene continued to welcome Elizabeth's visits. Finally, to Fred's surprise, the women's urgings began to wear him down and he started to think about going to church some—not all the time, just some. He didn't let them know it, though; it was best to keep that a secret. Then he did what he said he would never do. He started working graveyard. He didn't tell Irene and Elizabeth why, though. It was none of their business that he had decided to go to church. Again, to Fred's surprise, his graveyard job turned out to be a good and important job: setting up the machines for the next day's work.

"Fred," Irene said one day, "Pastor Thompson is preaching at a revival meeting down in Richmond next week. I really would like to go."

Now she wants to go all the way to Kentucky to church. Will she never give up? But Fred knew the answer. No, not Irene. Persistence was one of the qualities he liked best about her, but right now, he wasn't sure it was working in his favor.

He would think about it, he told Irene. And he did. In fact, he couldn't stop thinking about. That night at work, Fred tried to crowd out Irene's request with other thoughts. The Cincinnati Reds had lost several games recently and if they didn't shape up soon, they'd be out of the pennant race. The kitchen faucet was leaking and Fred couldn't fix it until he went to the hardware store for a replacement part; he'd go tomorrow.

But no matter what he tried to think about, his mind always returned to the same thing: A visit to Richmond would hurt nothing and it would be a good chance for a little vacation with Irene. It would make her happy and he might enjoy it, too.

When he told Irene they would go, she was delighted.

The church was packed. The preacher gave his sermon and then asked people who wanted prayer to come up front. In the prayer line that formed, Fred noticed a woman with a goiter. It was a relatively common sight in the days before iodized salt began to augment diets deficient in iodine. The woman's thyroid had enlarged substantially. For the bulge on her throat to be the size of a small adult's fist, the lump had been growing for quite some time.

Okay, God, Fred said silently, *I'll follow you if you heal that lady.* It was almost a dare, Fred's version of Gideon's fleece—an attempt to get God to give him a sign like the one God gave the biblical Gideon.

The preacher anointed the woman's forehead with oil, closed his eyes, and began to pray aloud. As Fred and the others watched, the goiter suddenly started shrinking and then disappeared, leaving no trace on the woman's throat.

Fred was astonished! He couldn't believe what he had seen and he couldn't *not* believe it! Neither could the ecstatic woman, who repeatedly stroked her newly normal throat, both laughing and crying as tears of joy ran down her cheeks.

After the service, Fred and Irene drove to their motel and quietly went to bed. The healing they had witnessed was not a common occurrence, but they said little about it. The drive back to Dayton the next day was mostly silent, too, with both of them consciously avoiding the subject neither of them dared approach.

Fleece

The rest of the week, Fred kept to himself the promise he had made to God, but he didn't forget it. When it was time to go to church, he couldn't wait to get there, and when the minister gave the altar call, Fred couldn't wait to respond. Going forward to the altar, he knelt and gave himself to Christ, promising always to follow him.

When he arose, there stood Elizabeth, the bane of Fred's existence. She was the very person he least wanted to see and the one he most needed to see. With great apprehension, he apologized for all the unkind things he had ever said about her. With no apprehension, she accepted his apology, complete with hugs and tears of joy.

Fred had put out a fleece, and when a real God produced a real sign, Fred turned and followed him—the forgiver and the forgiven harmonious at last. Like Fred and Elizabeth.

- -

Fred Coates later followed God's lead into the ministry, attending Dayton Bible Institute and working graveyard while grabbing sleep and study time as he could. Spurred by the same remarkable determination it took to work his way through school while supporting a family, he served more than 40 years as a pastor in three different states, once serving a church where Elizabeth was a member. Now retired, Fred has successfully battled separate episodes of prostate and esophageal cancer, and sustained the loss of his beloved Irene in June 2005. At age 85, he is still cancer free and is a senior companion volunteer at a nursing home in upper Michigan. He credits his long life to hard work, the blessing of modern medicine, and the miracle of God's healing power.

Butterfly

*Peace I leave with you; my peace I give you. I do
not give to you as the world gives. Do not let your
hearts be troubled and do not be afraid.*
John 14:27

Scary first days of school belong to kindergartners.
Unless you are an adult seminary student and college is
years behind you. And you have no friends nearby and no
money. And home is miles behind and your mother has
abandoned you—or at least it feels that way.

"Wait, come back," shouted Vallerie, flailing her arms
and running after the car. "I've made a mistake; come
back." Her words vanished like puffs of smoke as the car
grew smaller in the distance and finally disappeared around
a curve in the road.

Her mother and brother had left her and Vallerie was
terribly and utterly alone. The unspoken doubts that had
been building up in her mind all afternoon now filled up
her heart. Dwarfed by the red brick seminary dormitory that
was to be her home for the next three years, she stood in the
shadow of the building, breathless from running and feeling
terribly foolish. And very afraid.

Like a person who trips and harmlessly falls, and then
self-consciously looks around to see whether anyone else
has witnessed his embarrassment, Vallerie cautiously
glanced around to see whether anyone had seen her chasing
after the car. No, no one. Relieved, Vallerie turned to go
inside, reminding herself why she had come here.

She had been a college graduate with a good job, good
friends, and a good life, if not an overly prosperous one,
when she had responded to God's leading to enter the

Christian ministry. She had grown up in the church and loved everything about it—the worship, the music, the prayer, the Bible study, the group activities, the service projects. And she loved the people.

Vallerie knew, of course, that church members are not perfect, that uncomfortable disagreements sometimes develop in the group, and that people sometimes complain about one another and grumble about the pastor. But she also knew that these things did not represent the prevailing mood of the church or most of its people. She would deal with whatever she needed to and she trusted God to help her. She was committed to him and to the purpose of the church, and she looked forward to a life of service.

She had moments of uncertainty, of course, as she prepared to leave her home and family in Maryland and move to Kentucky to study at a seminary where she knew no one. Could she find part-time work to support herself while she was in school? Could she make friends? Could she handle the academic work after being out of an educational environment for years? What if she managed to graduate and then could not find work? Many churches in her denomination were not yet ready to accept women in positions of leadership. She would have fewer opportunities than would male seminary graduates. But her doubts always faded into the background as she listened to God and talked to herself. It would not be easy, but yes, she could do it.

Now clear that her mother and brother were not coming back, Vallerie trudged wearily upstairs to her room, silently repeating to herself what she no longer believed: *I can do it; yes, I can.*

Empty words, false words, untrue. In her small room, the words bounced off the walls and filled up her head with terrifying clatter like rocks thrown at wild dogs. Overwhelmed by panic, she rushed outside, feeling only that if she stayed inside, the walls would crush her as the room grew smaller and smaller.

Running wildly down the street, Vallerie could not outrun her panic. She crossed over onto the seminary lawn and followed an asphalt path down a small hill to a place she would later learn was called "the valley of decision." This scenic vale hosted several large shade trees and a small stream spanned by a charming stone footbridge where many seminary lovers had proposed and promised marriage. Out of breath and unaware of the valley's reputation for romance, she seated herself on the waist-high wall of the bridge and claimed it as a place of prayer.

Oh, God, what am I going to do? I was mad to come here. I can't do this! Powerless to help herself, her tears, thoughts, and words melded together as she sat dangling her feet off the side of the bridge.

How much time passed she did not know, but when she finally lifted her eyes, a small yellow butterfly flitted by. First, it darted away, and then returned. What type of butterfly was it, Vallerie wondered, idly wishing she had given her college zoology class more attention. Closer and closer the butterfly came, circling round and round, God's beautiful creature visiting her as it went about its butterfly business.

What proves God's transforming power more than a butterfly? What embodies more peace? What fulfills more promise? If God can transform a caterpillar into a butterfly, surely he can transform an adult seminary student into a Christian minister. A sense of wellbeing, authentic and reassuring, spread throughout Vallerie's body, melting her fear like ice cubes in sunlight. Refreshed and recommitted in the warmth of God's presence, and feeling a sense of peace as strong as the panic that earlier had chased her out of her room in terror, Vallerie arose and returned to the dorm to finish unpacking.

I can do this, she thought. Only this time, she meant it. She was exactly where God wanted her. He would help her and now she knew that. No panic, only peace.

The years of study and work passed, and every time Vallerie encountered difficulties along the way, she returned to the same stone footbridge in the same valley of decision. And without fail, every time she went there, a butterfly appeared.

- -

Vallerie King graduated from seminary and, along with her degree, received a coveted and prestigious honors award for her preaching. At this writing, she is pastor of Emmaus Baptist Church in Quinton, Virginia. Another of her experiences is told in "Birds."

Phone

My sheep listen to my voice; I know them,
and they follow me.
John 10:27

A ringing phone in the middle of the night means bad news. Except when it doesn't.

Mary was a Christian and had been since her baptism at age nine. She was young then, but she was old enough to know that she loved Jesus and wanted always to love him. What she didn't know was that Jesus wanted her to take up her cross daily and follow him (Luke 9:23). Still, for a few years, she was faithful in Sunday school and church attendance.

Then when she started junior high, she began to stray. She wasn't a bad girl and she wasn't doing bad things. She was just a teenager with a changing body and changing interests that didn't include the church.

Her church, a big church in relatively small Madisonville, is a church with a friendly small town Kentucky atmosphere. Someone always seemed to notice Mary's absence and let her know she was missed. Her intention was to return, but something always seemed to interfere. If Mary had been asked, she would have been unable to give a reason for gradually dropping out. It just happened. She drifted, developing a different group of friends and doing other things on Sunday until she eventually attended church only on Christmas and Easter.

But that was before the phone rang.

176

The night had started like any other. Now a senior in high school, Mary was tired. If she didn't give up and go to bed, she would oversleep the next morning and be late for school.

She loved her bedroom, especially now that she had her very own phone. Well, not exactly her phone; it belonged to her brother. In the era before cell phones, he had left it in his room when he went away to college. Finders, keepers; losers, weepers! Mary stretched the cord out the doorway and down the hall and moved the phone, which had its own separate line and separate listing, into her room.

Never has anyone coveted privacy more than a teenage girl! Conspiratorial conversations with friends, giggling about what Mrs. Barker had said in history class and gossiping about who was going out with whom, were conducted beyond the prying ears of parents. The privacy was delicious!

Mary's preparations for bed were routine. She brushed her teeth and removed her makeup—Oh, how she loved wearing makeup now that she was in high school!—undressed and put on her pajamas. She pulled out the stem on the back of the clock to activate the alarm, crawled into bed and pulled up the covers, and then turned off the lamp beside the phone on her bedside table. Tucking the covers underneath her chin, she settled down and closed her eyes. Long deep sigh. Asleep in seconds.

Hours later, the jangling phone awoke Mary. Fumbling around in the dark, the room black except for a dim streak of light spilling through a crack where the curtains failed to overlap in the middle of the window, she picked up the receiver. "Hello," she mumbled groggily.

"Is this the house where Mary Brown lives?"

Yes," said Mary to the unfamiliar female voice.

"Well, wake her up," said the woman. "It's ten after four."

"Okay," Mary said, in the confused fog of sleepiness uncertain whether to identify herself or not. She didn't. Automatically, she placed the phone back in its cradle and looked at the lighted dial of the clock. It was exactly 4:10 AM.

Blinking in a fruitless effort to banish the cloud of sleep from her eyes, she fingered the knobs on the back of the clock. The alarm stem was pushed in! Too drowsy to puzzle about what had happened, Mary pulled the stem out and fell back to sleep.

The alarm awoke her on time that morning and she remembered the incident clearly. She told her family and friends about it, but they understood it no better than she did. Unable to dismiss it from her mind, the more she thought about it the stranger it seemed.

Why hadn't the woman identified herself? Why hadn't Mary asked for the woman's name? Absent that, why hadn't Mary identified herself? How had the stranger known Mary's name? Why had the woman thought it necessary for Mary to know the time? How had the woman known Mary needed to be awakened? How had the stem for the alarm gotten pushed in during the night? How had the woman known the phone number to reach Mary? Everyone who knew her used the phone number listed in her parents' names, not the one listed in her brother's name. In fact, no one except her parents knew that Mary had moved her brother's phone into her room.

Two days later, Mary lay on the floor in her bedroom gazing at the ceiling and contemplating what had happened. Still puzzled, she couldn't let go of her questions. Then came the still small voice deep within her. *I'm watching after you,* said God.

Mary's questions vanished like the pretty lady from a magician's trunk. Mary didn't know who the caller was, how she knew the phone number to reach Mary, or how the caller knew that Mary would sleep late that morning if the alarm didn't sound. The only thing Mary knew was that God was calling her back to a faithful walk with him. He had been watching out for her, and he had used the phone call to tell her so—even when she was asleep, and even when she had strayed from him the way a sheep strays from a shepherd.

How is it that a pastor can speak hundreds of thousands of words over the years and one sentence can be unforgettable? "He comes to us," her pastor had said, "long before we recognize the need to come to him."

Mary didn't know she needed God, but he knew. And when he called her on the phone to tell her so, like the sheep with their shepherd, she heard his voice. And followed.

- -

Mary Allard followed the good Shepherd back to church and became active in youth choir and other youth activities. Today a wife, mother, and public school teacher, she still follows the good Shepherd. Two other of her experiences are told in "Headlights" and "Drummer."

Birds

*But ask the animals, and they will teach you, or the
birds of the air, and they will tell you....*
Job 12:7

The pale horse headed in Howard's direction. Steadily
and tirelessly, with a persistence born of absolute certainty,
death began to trot. Vallerie, fully aware of the clatter of
distant hoofs, noted her apprehension. She was not
concerned about her father's destination, only about his
journey.

She was his firstborn daughter and the oldest of five
children. Theirs had been a family paradoxically stable in
its instability. Vallerie and her siblings had known with
certainty that their mother would always be there no matter
what, but they had never known what to expect of their
father, who was captive to the vacillating ups and downs of
a manic depressive mood disorder. After decades of dealing
with the unpredictability of her husband's mental state,
only partially controlled by medication, Vallerie's mother a
year ago had passed peacefully into the arms of God.

Howard, now in his 70s, had never fully recovered from
the loss. His multiple ailments and their differing
medications now conspired against one another to
complicate medical treatment of his failing health. Bedfast,
he required round-the-clock care.

Vallerie sat by Howard's bedside praying and chatting
with him as he grew weaker. But his will to live was strong,
and she felt relatively comfortable leaving him to go to her
annual pre-arranged week of spiritual retreat.

The monastery was just as Vallerie remembered it, serene and restful. The cloistered halls of the retreat center called her to quietness of mind even as the tranquil beauty of the surrounding natural environment called her to stillness of heart. Temporarily withdrawing from her everyday life as a pastor, Vallerie prayed for peace for her father's journey and peace for herself in it.

Seated one day at the desk in her sparsely furnished room, Vallerie silently gazed out the window as a glistening white dove flashed across the sky and gently settled on the waiting branch of a ginkgo tree. Both the ancient dove and the ginkgo, the oldest living tree sometimes called a "living fossil," are living testimony to the staying power of God's created order. Vallerie thought it appropriate that the survivor of 250 million years should shelter a descendant of the first bird mentioned in the Bible.

It also was appropriate because it was the second time the universal symbol of peace had signaled God's answer to prayer as Vallerie approached the death of a loved one. The first time was on the day her mother would later die. Driving to her mother's bedside, Vallerie was waiting for a traffic light to change when a shimmering white dove, highlighted by the gleaming sun, circled round and round above her car carrying a message of peace on its wings. Now that it was Howard's time, the dove at the monastery reaffirmed the first dove's message: "Peace, deep peace of a loving God to you."

Her week of retreat at the monastery over, Vallerie returned home, where she began her drive to the hospital. Suddenly, two wild geese swept across the horizon in front of her car. Striking in their togetherness, they fluttered gracefully out of sight—two elegant partners on the wing. And when she arrived at the hospital, two geese—the same two geese, Vallerie thought—sat perched on the canopy above the semicircle driveway at the front entrance waiting for her arrival. Vallerie knew what it meant. Her mother was coming for her father, coming to show him the way, coming to take him with her where illness could never again cause them unhappiness.

But it was not yet Howard's time, and he lingered.

The next Sunday on her way to church, Vallerie sought God's assurance that she could put aside her preoccupation with her father's decline long enough to focus on her responsibilities for the day. Suddenly, a soft but very recognizable sound startled her: the low haunting "Hoo, hoo" of an unseen owl. A nocturnal creature calling out in broad daylight? Yes, and Vallerie understood the message this common symbol of wisdom carried: Wisdom that comes from heaven is pure (James 3:17). It was becoming a pattern now for God to use one of his winged creatures from heaven to remind Vallerie that he was with her and with her father.

The next week, she sat through the night by Howard's bedside as he passed through death's door into life eternal. As the rising sun filled the room with the first light of dawn, birds in the trees outside the window raised their voices in chorus and filled the room with glorious music— heavenly sunlight accompanied by heavenly birdsong. What could be a more fitting postlude from one life, a more appropriate prelude to another? Sunlight and birdsong— exquisite escorts for Howard's passage.

But just as death is a passage, so is grief, and Vallerie's was just beginning. The next Sunday on her way to church, she keenly felt her loss. Pulling her car off the road, she threw herself on God's compassion, reaffirming her trust that he was with her. When she raised her eyes, there they were—bluebirds. Radiantly beautiful bluebirds, luminously brilliant bluebirds, stunningly striking bluebirds. Never before had Vallerie seen real ones, these traditional symbols of happiness: a heavenly sign that her father now was happy and never again would be unhappy. And that knowledge was just what she needed to smooth the jagged edge off her sense of loss.

It is said that birds befriended St. Francis of Assisi and brought him messages from God. Perhaps birds developed a special language during their association with the patron saint of animals. For in the autumn of her father's passage, the birds of the air brought Vallerie messages from God. And every time, they told her of his love.

- -

Vallerie King is still pastor of the church that actively supported her during her father's illness and following his death. Another of Vallerie's experiences in told in "Butterfly."

Arms

Place me like a seal over your heart, like a seal on your arm; for love is as strong as death.
Song of Songs 8:6

A boy who loses a father becomes a man who lost a father. The boy doesn't change how he feels about it; he just grows up.

Gail knew this because she married the man. Chris never complained about losing his father and he never saw himself as a victim. He didn't have a father; that's all. His dad had died when Chris was 10. Chris had missed spending time with his father, and he said that. And that was about *all* he said about it.

But Gail, the woman who fell in love with the man, knew that Chris had missed something he wanted and needed. Not that Chris's mom had been a bad parent; in fact, she had been a good mother. Still, Chris had missed his dad.

Chris had wondered over the years how different his life would have been had his dad lived. Would he have come to watch Chris's high school basketball games the way he came to watch his Little League games? Would he have taught Chris to drive a car? Would he have talked to Chris about how to relate to girls so he would have felt less awkward when he began to take an interest in them? Would he have talked to him about—you know, things fathers talk to their sons about?

Chris did not have the answers to these questions but he had his memories, which he treasured. His father had loved Chris and Chris knew that. It didn't make up for all the things they could have done together had his father lived, but it made up for a lot.

One of the first things Gail noticed when she married Chris was that he always slept on his back with his arms folded across his chest. To Gail, he looked as if he were laid out in a casket ready for burial. "Hey, Chris," she would tease. "You dead in there?"

"No, not yet," he would respond, laughing. "You gettin' your hopes up?"

"Nope, I know you're not going anywhere important," she would reply smiling. "I can see that you don't have on your suit and tie." And to Gail, it truly was a joke, a personal preference no more important than on which side of the bed Chris felt comfortable sleeping.

Had the fly on the wall been a psychologist, it might have speculated that Chris's sleeping position was one of defense. Weapons are called arms for a reason. They can extend the reach of the upper limbs of the body and hold an enemy farther away than can natural arms. Used offensively or defensively, arms—either biological or manufactured—can protect the body's vital organs. In body language, arms crossed across the chest can signify a subconscious need to protect the heart from the pain of emotional loss.

To Chris and Gail, his sleeping position was none of these things. Some people favor sleeping in a fetal position, some favor one side or the other, and some favor their back. Leave the analysis to psychologists.

One night, Gail awoke from a sound sleep to find the room bathed in a dim light, soft and diffused. And someone was in the room with Chris and her. How Gail knew that she wasn't sure. She couldn't see the person, she just felt his presence. And she was frightened.

Rolling over, she saw Chris sleeping soundly on the right side of their bed. And beside Chris on the bed sat a male figure with his hands on top of Chris's hands as his arms lay folded across his chest.

Oh! It's Chris's dad, thought Gail. She couldn't see the face of the figure, but she had seen photos of Chris's father, and the build of the figure and the tilt of his head were exactly like the photos she had seen. Yes, it was Chris's father!

Gail gasped and Chris awoke. Instantly, the figure vanished like wispy smoke in a summer shower, taking Gail's fear with it. "Your dad was here sitting beside you," she said, recalling that his dad's birthday was approaching—an occasion that Chris mentioned every year on October 23.

Gail's statement might have surprised someone else, but Chris knew Gail too well to be surprised. He was aware that his wife had a remarkable way of sometimes knowing things she had no logical way of knowing, and that sometimes she knew things before they happened.

Like the time Gail had begun to cry uncontrollably. She wasn't sure why she was crying, except that she felt something horrific was happening to someone she knew. Later, she learned that a friend's husband had been killed in an automobile accident at exactly the time Gail was crying.

Another time, Gail had known the exact date and time of her sister-in-law's death, and even the color of the dress in which she would be buried—and she had told Chris these things about his sister before they happened. "Got any lottery numbers for us?" teased Gail's nieces when they learned of their aunt's prediction. Wouldn't it be nice if Gail's ability to predict the future would extend to the winning lottery numbers and she would give the numbers to them?

Other similar experiences had occurred, and Chris had learned to take Gail's unusual abilities in stride, just as she did. She seldom spoke of them, and when she did, she spoke in a remarkably unassuming manner. She was a Christian and she gave God credit for everything good that happened. If he gave Gail special spiritual gifts, it was because of his own reasons, not because she sought them. Sometimes these abilities prepared her for someone's approaching death. Other times, she was allowed to help people who were facing death and those who loved them. If there were a gift, it was the gift of helping others, not of knowing things she had no logical way of knowing.

So when Gail told Chris that she had seen his father sitting beside him on the bed, even though Chris had never before heard her talk about witnessing anything similar, Chris's first response was not disbelief that it could happen, but acceptance. "How do you know it was Dad?" he asked.

Gail was familiar with the seventeenth chapter of Matthew. Moses and Elijah, long after they were dead, appeared to Jesus, and three witnesses—Peter, James, and John—witnessed the event. If God let Moses and Elijah cross the bridge between heaven and earth, perhaps God would allow other heavenly residents to cross it, too. "I just know," replied Gail. "I feel that your father needed to see you, and you have received a wonderful blessing."

But if God had let Chris's father come back to see Chris, God must have had a reason. What was it? And why did God let Chris's father show himself to Gail instead of to Chris? Gail didn't know and she didn't think it important. What was important was that Chris experience his father's blessing.

Arms

Open heart, open arms. The parallel is so obvious that only the most obtuse person can miss it. Poets rhapsodize about it. Musicians sing about it. Writers elaborate about it. But none of them has told the story of the night Chris's father returned to lay healing hands on the heart of his son.

Yes, it was a blessing, and Chris no longer sleeps on his back with his arms folded across his chest. For on one special night in a room softly bathed in light, a father's love was as strong as death.

- -

Gail Hylton, Fredericksburg, Virginia, is Area Coordinator with Hopetree Ministries, which manages the two residential facilities for people with disabilities mentioned in "Wings." Chris Hylton is a teacher in Stafford County, Virginia, public schools.

Voicemail

And the peace of God, which transcends all
understanding, will guard your hearts and your
minds in Christ Jesus.
Philippians 4:7

The divorce that left a gaping wound in Rhonda's heart also left a vacant room in her house. With space to spare and Rhonda's mother getting on in years, the two of them decided that it was time for Margaret to come to live with Rhonda.

It was a good thing; their bond was close and they did many things together. They took their meals together; they went to church together. They shopped for groceries together; they watched TV together. They took a trip to the Holy Land; they took a trip to Disney World.

One day after work, Rhonda went straight from her office to a finance committee meeting at church and then drove home. Pulling her car into the driveway, she noticed it immediately. The house was dark.

Hurrying up the walk, she opened the door and stepped inside. "Mom?" she called, switching on a light. No answer.

Rhonda's heart quickened.

Flipping on more lights, she hurried down the hallway and entered Margaret's room. There Rhonda found her mother lying in bed in the same position as when Rhonda had left for work that morning. The bed covers were completely undisturbed; Margaret had not moved. *Oh, dear God!*

The next moments were a blur. Even before she touched Margaret, Rhonda knew her mom was gone. Even before she felt sadness, she felt shock. Even before she felt decisive, she felt confusion.

Be calm, Rhonda, be calm.

Quickly she grabbed a phone and punched in the numbers for her pastor's cell. On his way home from the same finance committee meeting Rhonda had just attended, Dr. Bob was immediately responsive. He rushed to his house a few doors down the street from Rhonda, collected his wife, and within minutes, both he and Katherine were standing in Rhonda's entrance hall wrapping her in a comforting embrace.

Thank God for good pastors! Quietly and calmly, Dr. Bob took charge while Katherine comforted Rhonda. Emergency medical technicians, summoned by Rhonda's 911 call, routinely went about their business while Oscar, Rhonda's pet tiger cat, silently paced the floor feeling lost in the shuffle. He had been in the house all day without human companionship, a circumstance as unusual for him as was the commotion of the coming and going of strangers in the middle of the night. Something was amiss and Oscar sensed it.

Rhonda's mom probably had passed in her sleep, said the EMTs, telling Rhonda what she already knew. Then they told her something she didn't know. From all appearances, Margaret had died about nine that morning.

After one more phone call, attendants from the funeral home took Rhonda's mother away. Dr. Bob and Katherine sat with Rhonda around the kitchen table, reviewing the events of the day and making plans for the next steps while Oscar, curled up in Rhonda's lap, slept comfortably. For the moment, the pastor and his wife had done all they could; it was time for them to go.

Rising from the table, Dr. Bob and Katherine grasped hands, each taking one of Rhonda's hands as she remained seated. Forming an intimate circle of three around the table, they bowed their heads to pray. Then, in a move that would forever endear Oscar to Rhonda, he sat up in her lap and pressed his head against Katherine and Rhonda's linked hands. Adamantly insisting that he be included, he retained the pressure against their clasped hands during a long prayer. *I'm a part of the family and I've lost somebody, too,* he seemed to be saying. *And I need a blessing.*

Worse things can happen in time of trouble than being owned by a cat.

Dr. Bob and Katherine left, and at one thirty in the morning, Rhonda was not ready for bed. She picked up the phone to check her voicemail, mentally noting that the day had unexpectedly morphed into what seemed like an endless night. Punching in her pass code, she waited. Yes, a message had been left at nine on that crucial morning. Entering the "listen" code, Rhonda heard a one-syllable message. "Peace," said a high-pitched feminine voice.

Peace? Rhonda looked at the receiver quizzically, as if her puzzlement could squeeze out its secret. She listened to the message again, and then again, replaying it several times. Yes, the word was "peace." But who was the woman? Rhonda's mind began to churn, dismissing thoughts almost as soon as they appeared.

It was the voice of her mother. No, it was not the voice of her mother. Rhonda would have known that voice anywhere. Anyway, Margaret couldn't have called the home phone while she was at home—duh!

Voicemail

It was the voice of a business acquaintance. No, it was not the voice of a business acquaintance. If it were, she would have left her number to receive a return call.

It was a message left by mistake. No, it was not a message left by mistake. Anyone who dialed Rhonda's number in error would have recognized the mistake as soon as Rhonda's recorded greeting played, and either would have hung up without leaving a message or would have excused herself and then hung up.

It was a crank call. No, it was not a crank call. A crank caller would have left a crank message, not a purposeful one.

It was a purposeful message? Yes, and one God knew Rhonda needed: a message of peace. But why a feminine voice?

And why not? God is spirit, neither male nor female. "He" is simply the default pronoun used when language has no gender-neutral pronoun to identify a person. If God can speak in a masculine voice at one time, God can speak in a feminine voice at another time. Perhaps the situation determines the voice. One thing is certain. The gender of the listener did not determine the gender of the voice, because Rhonda saved the message for days and allowed friends of both genders to listen to it. They all heard a female voice, and no one had a better explanation for the message than Rhonda did. Finally, after two weeks, the phone company automatically deleted the recording.

Comforted by the message, Rhonda moved through the necessary tasks of the next days and weeks completely at peace. Yes, she grieved the loss of her mother, but she did not grieve as those who have no hope (I Thessalonians 4:13-14). Her mother had passed from this world to the next in peace, and Rhonda accepted her mother's passing in peace.

And when asked why she didn't try to trace the call to find its origin, Rhonda explained it easily. She had no need to trace the call. God doesn't have a phone number. He answers prayers, not phones.

- -

At the request of the contributor, the names used in this story are fictitious.

Roadblock

*...your Father knows what you need
before you ask him.
Matthew 6:8*

He needed some traffic cones. Five traffic cones, to be exact. It didn't seem too much to ask. Traffic cones were as necessary as traffic lights, and almost as common. Just the other day, Richard had seen a short stack of traffic cones stashed on the front bumper of a local utility truck. Who would think these unsightly roadblocks of street construction would be so hard to find?

It was all because of the driveway. It had taken more than its share of use, if not abuse, from the 40 years of ins and outs of five family members and four cars. Oh, the joys of home ownership!

Richard called a few contractors, took bids, and selected a business to install a new driveway. Unwilling to shrug off the protection of the freshly poured concrete to a contractor who would leave before the concrete had dried and hardened, Richard determined to find a way to block traffic from the wet pavement that stretched across the pedestrian sidewalk in front of his house before emptying into the street.

If not for the abundance of neighborhood children, Richard would have been less concerned. But with an elementary school only three blocks away and a middle school seven blocks away, this suburban street received more than a typical share of traffic, both pedestrian and vehicular. The children would need protection as much as would the sidewalk.

On school days, Richard enjoyed watching the children. They dawdled along, backpacks stuffed with books and school supplies. Usually grouped haphazardly in small clusters, the kids sometimes stopped for brief moments of chatter before moving on, the little ones occasionally skipping a few steps or hopping across the cracks in the sidewalk. Rarely there would be a mild scuffle, but mostly, any physical contact was good-natured jostling.

The children would not notice the fresh concrete until they were on top of it. And when they noticed, they might be unable to resist the temptation to retrieve a stick from underneath a nearby tree, or a pencil from a school bag, and scratch their name or a tic-tac-toe grid in the pavement, or intentionally leave behind a handprint or footprint. The possibility of defacing property would not enter their minds. To them, it would not be mischief. They were children; they would behave as children.

Then, there were the bicyclists and skateboarders, mostly junior high boys. In the youthful exuberance of impulsive risk-taking, the bicyclists sped around the downhill curve on the run, different ones jockeying to the front as they raced one another to the end of the block. The skateboarders, mindful of their contrived edginess, barreled around the curve in their long baggy shorts, disdaining the use of protective gear as they hopped curbs, popped wheelies, and dreamed of curling a half pipe to catch air in a 360. The bicyclists and skateboarders would be on top of the fresh concrete before they saw it, not just damaging the new pavement but perhaps also taking a jarring spill.

No time to waste; the work crew was only a few days away. Richard phoned several potential suppliers of traffic cones. Their responses were the same, even if their words were different. No, we don't have any; maybe you should call the department of public works. No, we don't stock them; have you tried Home Depot? No, it never occurred to me; I wonder where people *do* get those things?

Construction sawhorses from a home supply store might have served the purpose, or several strategically placed outdoor chairs with colorful tape stretched between them the way police officers stretch yellow tape around an area to block off a crime scene. But Richard was focused on traffic cones, their bright day-glow orange more visible to the children as they rounded the downhill curve than sawhorses or yellow crime scene tape would be.

Meanwhile, Richard, for years a Christian and active church member, had been feeling distanced from God. "If you aren't close to God, guess who moved?" read a sign in a nearby churchyard. It was a stereotypical platitude and the average person would have sloughed it off, but Richard was not an average person. He took the message seriously and moved closer to God. The next morning before he went about his daily activities, he took time to pray, read his Bible, and contemplate the wonders of the God he served.

Then, idly gazing out his bedroom window toward the stream flowing along the boundary of his backyard about 20 feet away, he noticed a bright object—no, three bright objects. He moved closer to the window. Unbelievable! Three bright day-glow orange traffic cones were snagged in the rocks of the stream!

Excitedly, Richard donned a pair of khaki shorts and slipped into his old canvas deck shoes. His feet protected against the rocks in the creek, he sloshed out into the middle of the stream, the water covering his ankles. As he reached to salvage the cones, he idly glanced at the nearby spillway. And there, entangled in weeds that city workers had not yet cleared away in their ongoing effort to chase away the resident river otters, were two more traffic cones.

Environmental litter thoughtlessly abandoned after street reconstruction? Accidental debris washed down from the high school parking lot a few blocks upstream? Deliberate sabotage, the unwanted objects secretly trashed by vandals? One of these or some combination of them, what did it matter? It was tangible evidence that God knew what Richard needed even before he asked. The timing was perfect, the number exact.

Most people encounter a roadblock at some time, and usually, people don't like them. Richard loved his. And no, it wasn't a coincidence. It was a God incidence.

- -

Richard Parvin is retired and lives in Clearwater, Florida. Another of his experiences is told in "Parable."

Engraving

*...I will not forget you. See, I have engraved you
on the palms of my hands; your walls are ever
before me.*
Isaiah 49:15b-16

She never gave much thought to visions, except for those she read about in the Bible, or dreams, either. Dreams were similar to visions, except that dreams occurred when people were asleep and visions occurred when people were awake. Dreams were a routine part of everyday life and visions were—what? Not routine.

Twenty-six years ago, she had been diagnosed with diabetes. Since then, Donna had acquired many of the disorders that can accompany the disease: congestive heart failure, coronary artery disease, rheumatoid arthritis, chronic obstructive pulmonary disease, hypertension, orthostatic hypertension, renal disease, diabetic neuropathy, and diabetic retinopathy that had left her visually impaired.

Now, thanks to an accidental fall that required several surgical procedures to repair broken bones in her right foot, she was temporarily confined to a wheelchair. With two external fixator cages pinned in 18 different places in her foot and leg, even the simple acts of daily life were a challenge. Nighttime sleep was always slow to arrive, and to avoid insomnia, Donna had developed a habit of being sure that she felt drowsy before going to bed. Tonight she had waited until 1:00 AM.

Like the psalmist, Donna was worn out from calling for help (Psalm 69:3). Still, she couldn't sleep. Awake in the dark, she reviewed the difficulties of the day. Things had not always been this way, she reminded herself. She once

198

had been able bodied. Now she was desperate for God's help with even the smallest task. She prayed earnestly.

Suddenly, an image of two open hands appeared before Donna. Amazed, Donna glanced around the night-darkened room to reassure herself that she was completely awake. *See, I have engraved you on the palms of my hands,* she thought, remembering the scripture she had memorized. Immediately, she knew that the hands were those of Jesus. But instead of scars where the nails had pierced his body at the crucifixion, there were openings—wide ones through which Donna could see.

Donna saw herself step forward—no wheelchair, no halting gait—for a closer look. Through the openings in the palms of Jesus' hands, she saw a huge open book comprised of two columns of text extending as far as she could see.

Donna couldn't read the book. Was it because of her poor eyesight, or was it because the message did not pertain to her? As she strained forward, unconsciously squinting in an effort to read, one word separated itself from the text and moved closer to her. The word grew bigger as it came into focus, as if enlarged by a magnifying glass. It was her name!

Then somehow, as miraculous as the image itself, the text transformed from lettering on a page to lettering on a great white wall. Underneath Donna's name, in dark red ink as wet as when it flowed from the pen, streamed a list of the events of Donna's life from birth forward.

Donna Marie Price Davis, born May 23, 1951, to Bracyle Lewis Price and Ruby Evelyn Spencer Price. Donna's first day of school. Her baptism. Her graduation from high school. Her wedding. On and on went the writing. The words themselves seemed to have life.

Engraving
199

Supernaturally, somehow, Donna vividly relived her past through the various stages of life while she read and simultaneously contemplated the message.

Presently, Donna detected a slight hint of fragrance—incense, like the perfume the woman from Bethany brought to Jesus in an alabaster jar (Matthew 26:6-8). In literary terms, the account of the anointment of Jesus with fragrance was a foreshadowing of his future. In reality, it was a teachable moment, an occasion for Jesus to prepare his followers for what was to come. For after the crucifixion, Joseph of Arimathea and Nicodemus prepared Jesus for burial by applying a mixture of myrrh and aloe to the linen strips they wound around his body (John 19:38-40). The scent of the burial spices had remained—additional confirmation that the hands Donna saw were those of Jesus.

Still reading and reliving the events of her life, Donna noticed a streak of ink that covered previous writing, obscuring it and rendering the original message illegible. Then she realized that none of the bad things she had ever done were recorded on the wall. All her sins had been blotted out by the red ink: the blood of Jesus.

The longer Donna read, the more years passed. Still, her sinful acts did not appear in her personal history. Now in the present and still reading her life written on the wall, she reached the end of the unfinished script—unfinished because her life was unfinished.

Donna knew what the vision meant and why it had come in a manner that melded together the image of Isaiah's wall and Malachai's book of remembrance (Malachai 3:16) with her own experience. Years earlier, when Donna was physically able to hold a job, she had worked at Lawn View Apartments. She had permanently marked the project's belongings—keys, tools, lawn equipment—by placing a metal punch against the item and striking the punch with a hammer to engrave a code number in metal and wooden objects: 12 22—12 for L, the twelfth letter of the alphabet, and 22 for V, the twenty-second letter of the alphabet. Property engraved with 12 22 belonged to Lawn View Apartments.

Jesus' hands were marked like that, Donna thought. Every name written in the book of remembrance had been written on the nails that pierced his hands, engraving there for eternity the names of those who call him Lord.

Donna rolled over in bed and looked at the clock. It was 3:00 AM and she was very ill. By the time her husband answered her call, she was unresponsive. Her blood sugar measured 52, dangerously lower than normal; her blood pressure measured 72 over 43 as compared to a typical goal of 120 over 80. It took six hours of emergency room care to restore Donna to alertness.

Science has more than one theory to explain what happened to Donna. When death approaches, cerebral anoxia produces hallucinations due to a shortage of oxygen in the brain. Another possibility is that during a life-threatening situation, endorphins flood the brain and produce hallucinations as an avoidance response.

Donna is not concerned that there is a biological basis for her vision. This does not discount its content—one matching her experience and using scriptures she had committed to memory—nor minimize her interpretation of it. She belongs to God and her name is engraved on the palms of Jesus' hands. He remembers her name and forgets her sin.

Donna M. Davis lives in Shallotte, North Carolina. A year after this experience, she is out of the wheelchair and walking in a limited fashion.

Drummer

*... So they hurried off and found Mary and Joseph,
and the baby, who was lying in the manger... and all
who heard it were amazed at what the shepherds
said to them. But Mary treasured up all these things
and pondered them in her heart.*
Luke 2:16, 18-19

She didn't wind it. In fact, it hadn't been wound in years. She didn't even know whether the music box still worked. Not that it mattered; it was just a Christmas decoration casually placed on a living room table.

Frankly, Mary wasn't much into Christmas this year. She was just going through the motions. A graduate school paper was breathing down her neck, and she and Mike were preoccupied with the medical help they had sought in effort to conceive a child.

It had been a long road. Seven years earlier, after his first marriage had produced Bill and Millie, Mike had a vasectomy. But that was before he had the slightest suspicion that his marriage would fail, and before he found Mary, fell in love, and married again. The vasectomy that had once made sense to Mike no longer made sense. He and Mary dreamed of a child to bless their union. If only his vasectomy could be undone!

Such reversals were possible, Mike and Mary learned, and pregnancies sometimes resulted. But both of them were in graduate school, with the expectation that advanced credits would increase their income as public school teachers. Until they accrued the extra credits they needed, their limited income ruled out the expensive elective surgery necessary to reverse Mike's vasectomy.

Still, Mike was determined, and he finally found a reputable physician who agreed to perform the surgery for a reasonable price. Both Mike and Mary were delighted in July when the surgery was successfully completed. Caution was in order, though, warned the doctor. It could take four to six months for Mike's reproductive system to return to normal. Even then, the longer a vasectomy had been in place, the greater was the risk of infertility. Mike's chances of fathering another child were only fifty-fifty.

But his chances of finding the right doctor had been problematic, too, and Mike had found one. So he and Mary were prayerfully optimistic.

By the time Mike completed his Masters degree, Mary had only one more course to finish. Everything hinged on her getting her last paper submitted by December 12—the Monday after the Sunday evening worship service in which she was scheduled to sing in her church's Christmas cantata.

The only way Mary could meet her Sunday night responsibility was to stay at home on Sunday morning and finish her school paper. So Mike took Bill and Millie to morning worship, and since personal computers had not yet found their way into common usage, Mary settled down at the kitchen table with her typewriter.

As she worked, her mind darted between the paper she was typing and the worship service she was missing. She looked at her watch. It was ten-thirty, about time for the choir to head for the sanctuary.

Some minutes later, two unexplainable and unrelated events unfolded in separate places.

"Guess what?" said Mike that afternoon as the family sat down for lunch. "The choir sang 'The Little Drummer Boy' at church this morning."

Mary's eyes widened. "Really?" Then she launched into her story. Sometime after ten-thirty as she sat typing her paper, a faint metallic tune had wafted its way into the kitchen. She had turned toward the music box on top of the microwave. No, the sound was not coming from there.

Puzzled, Mary arose from her chair and wandered through the house, growing more curious the nearer she drew to the sound. Entering the living room, she felt wonder replace her curiosity. The music box, unwound for years, was spontaneously playing "The Little Drummer Boy." *Unbelievable*, thought Mary, kneeling in front of the music box to see it better. *I'm listening, God. What do you want to tell me?*

Mary nodded, Pa-rum-pa-pum-pum....[11]

"And God gave me a message," Mary excitedly told Mike and the children, omitting the details. "I can't prove it, but I think the music box played 'The Little Drummer Boy' at exactly the same time the choir sang it at church."

Different people later posed different explanations for what happened that morning, some reasons more spiritual than others. "Maybe it was God's way of bringing the worship service to you since you couldn't be there," said Mary's sister when she learned of the events.

Mary smiled. It was the most obvious explanation for why the implausible had happened, if not for how. But to Mary, it was more than that, for God had imprinted on her heart an unshakable message. Just as the little drummer boy in the legend had played his music for the Virgin Mary and the Baby she had born, the little drummer boy in the music box had played his music for Mary and the baby she would bear.

And just as the first century Mary kept secret the shepherds' message about her baby, the twentieth century Mary kept secret the little drummer boy's message about hers. Everybody else could wait to learn about her pregnancy, just as she would wait for medical confirmation. But unlike the others, she would wait expectantly.

- -

Nine months after the little drummer played his tune, Mary Allard bore a healthy baby girl. Two more of Mary's experiences with God appear in "Phone" and "Headlights."

Arch

And I—in righteousness I will see your face; when I awake, I will be satisfied with seeing your likeness.
Psalm 17:15

Jesus in the arch. It sounded like the name of a Christian rock band, or maybe the address of a Christian website, but without the www. It was neither.

"Come out here, Mom," shouted Beth. "You've got to see this."

"See what?" asked Pat, stepping out the front door of her apartment and standing beside Beth and Sarah on the porch.

"Jesus in the arch," said Beth, pointing. "See over there?"

Pat looked toward the main entrance to the three-story apartment building across the street. "Where? You mean in the center arch just beyond the palm tree?"

"Yeah, right there," said Beth, still pointing.

Sarah, Pat's niece and Beth's cousin, nodded. "Just keep looking," she said. "The face of Jesus will appear if you focus on the center of the arch at the main entrance."

Pat focused. Nothing. She squinted. Still nothing. What she was looking for she wasn't exactly sure, but she expected to see something like that well-known Heinrich Hoffman portrait, "Christ at Thirty-Three"—the bust of a brown-bearded kind-looking man who, by looking down, compelled people to look into his soul and truly see him.

Like a turtle peering out of its shell, Pat strained her neck forward. Her inelegant attempt to get a little closer to the image didn't help. She still couldn't see what her daughter and Sarah said they saw.

Sarah was a spiritual person. She wholeheartedly believed that God was all and in all, whether she saw a sign of his presence or not. Pat did, too, even if she didn't talk much about it. To her, more religious inside than she showed, faith was an intensely private matter. Jesus was in the heart, not in the arch. Still, if the other two women saw the image of Jesus in the arch, Pat wanted to see it, too.

But she didn't.

"It's right there," insisted Sarah, Pat and Beth's houseguest for the week.

Like most relationships, theirs had transitioned. Once the three had lived near one another in Indiana, but Pat had moved to Florida and Beth had joined her a few years later. Now the three stayed in touch by sharing greeting cards, emails, phone calls, and personal visits.

Back in Indiana, Sarah had been functioning on overload so long that her stressometer, if there had been such a thing, was over the top. She loved her nine-year-old twin boys beyond measure, but there were times when their level of activity was double trouble. She and her husband still had a mountain of debt from the costs of the in vitro fertilization that gave them the boys. She lived with chronic pain from Complex Regional Pain Syndrome, a neurological condition in which nerve injury—sometimes of unknown origin—produces burning pain, pathological changes in bone and skin, tissue swelling, and extreme sensitivity to touch. Her medical insurance had run out, and on top of all that, she was a member of the sandwich generation, looking after her aging mother along with her immediate family.

The only thing that enabled her to cope was God and his everlasting love. Even so, Sarah urgently needed a respite and some spiritual reinforcement.

"Come on down," Pat had said on the phone. "It's warm down here in Clearwater, and a change of scenery will do you good. Beth and I are only twenty minutes from the beach. We'll eat whatever we want, and as much of it as we want. And we won't feel guilty or ask anybody's permission. And we'll do touristy things and go shopping at the mall. We don't have to spend money, we can window shop. And when we get tired, we'll just veg out."

It's either Florida or a mental hospital, thought Sarah. Easy pick—Florida. And before she left Indiana, she talked to God about everything. She didn't ask for healing or money or health insurance. She asked for spiritual help. "And, please, God," she said, "if possible, show me a sign that you are with me."

So there Sarah was, vegging out on Pat and Beth's front porch when she looked up and saw the image of Jesus in the entry arch of the apartment building across the street. The image was difficult to describe, but it was a shadowy form created by the way the branch of a nearby tree followed the curve of the arch, and the way the tree's leaves draped the inside curve of the arch, and—and when Sarah called Beth outside, Beth saw the image, too. The image that Pat couldn't see.

What's the matter with me? Pat wondered, recalling the famous sighting of an image of the Virgin Mary right there in Clearwater. In December 1996, someone discovered the image on the outside glass wall of a bank building. Within days, tens of thousands of people flocked to the site. Nearby merchants hawked tee shirts and trinkets, Clearwater police assigned a squad of officers to direct foot and vehicular traffic, and the city formed a Miracle Management Task Force to deal with the crowd. Detractors said that the rainbow-tinted shape resembling a stylized image of the Virgin Mary was nothing more than a water stain from an irrigation sprinkler that blew out its nozzle and showered the glass-paneled side of the bank building. In 1997, vandals sprayed the image with acid, badly staining and obscuring a large portion of it. But a month later, a downpour washed away the stain and the image re-emerged. Many of the faithful who saw it said that it gave them happiness, and some reported healings of physical illnesses.[12]

Was this reported image a hoax? Was there a natural explanation? Or was it a miracle, God acting to give people reason to notice him? Pat didn't know. She had seen the image and had read about other similar sightings in different places. An image of the Virgin Mary holding baby Jesus reportedly had appeared on the window of a Boston hospital. An image of the Virgin Mary reportedly had appeared on a toasted cheese sandwich auctioned on eBay for a sum of $28,000. Similar sightings around the world were numerous and had been widely documented over many years. These reports were matters of momentary curiosity for Pat, not matters for scientific or religious inquiry. She was a no-nonsense practical person and she didn't waste time trying to answer unanswerable questions.

But hearing strangers say they saw an image of the Virgin Mary on the glass wall of a bank building in the business district did not carry the same weight with Pat as hearing her daughter and her niece say they saw an image of Jesus in the entry arch of the apartment building across the street. "Where are you going?" asked Pat as Beth turned to go inside.

"Wait and see," said Beth, quickly returning with her sophisticated digital camera. Aiming it, she clicked the button several times. Why she took the photos, she didn't know. She was an excellent photographer. She understood about perspective and point of view, and light and shadow, and the phenomenon of optical illusion. For her, snapping a photo was the natural thing to do. "See?" said Beth, pressing the button on the viewer and holding it up for her mother to see.

There it was, the image of Jesus in the photo! Now that Pat saw it clearly, it wasn't like the Heinrich Hoffman portrait at all. This was a semi-profile bust of a longhaired, quietly contemplative bearded man positioned next to one side of the arch and facing the other side. And when Pat looked toward the arch, she saw the image there, too. Why she had not seen it before she didn't know, any more than she knew why she saw it now, except that there it was. And during the next few days when Beth took more photos at various times of day and night, there it still was.

As mystified as Pat was by this unexplained sighting, that's how enraptured Sarah was. She had asked God for a sign of his presence and he had sent it. She felt better now, her worries about her personal problems less acute and her struggle with how she could handle them relieved. A few days later when she stepped onto the plane to fly back to Indiana, Sarah felt less burdened by her future and more able to manage whatever uncertainties it held.

One thing Pat knew. This sighting was not like the others. Not like the image she had seen on the wall of the bank building in Clearwater. Not like the image she had read about on the window of the hospital in Boston. Not like the image on the toasted cheese sandwich sold on eBay. No, the image of Jesus in the arch across the street was different. It had not gained media attention, had not attracted gawking sightseers that disrupted the neighborhood, and had not separated people from their money in exchange for a cheap trinket that exploited their faith. The image of Jesus in the arch across the street had come after a specific prayer request, had appeared to only three witnesses, and had stayed only long enough to do its job: assure Sarah of God's presence.

Sarah talked little about it. She was satisfied simply to have seen the likeness of Jesus. As for Pat, when the episode was over, it was over—as much mystery as reality. She didn't care; she believed. Jesus in the arch *and* Jesus in the heart.

- -

Patricia Focht still lives in the same apartment building in Clearwater, Florida, and Beth has moved away. A few days after Sarah Schuler returned home to Williamsburg, Indiana, Beth phoned to say that the image of Jesus in the arch had disappeared. "Thank God for cameras," said Sarah who still treasures the photos Beth snapped. As a part of Sarah's faith testimony, she shares the photos with others, including the author, who relied on both day and night images of the scene for her description of Jesus in the arch.

End Notes

[1] **Introduction.** *Spiritual and Religious Transformation in America: The National Spiritual Transformation Study*, December 8, 2005; http://www-news.uchicago.edu/releases/05/121305.norc.pdf, accessed March 28, 2008.

[2] **Introduction.** The Christian Ethics Today Foundation, ©2000-2008, www.christianethicstoday.com/Issue/053/Dr.%King, accessed March 31, 2008.

[3] **Introduction.** "Leading A Religion That Lacks a Creed," *Perspective*, Bill Maxwell, *St. Petersburg Times*, p. 4A, April 11, 2008.

[4] **Play.** "I Saw The Light," © Copyright 1948 Hank Williams Sr., renewed 1975 Acuff-Rose Music, Inc.

[5] **Play.** "The Barefoot Boy," John Greenleaf Whittier, 1855, http://holyjoe.org.poetry/whittier.htm, accessed June 2, 2009.

[6] **Feather.** William P. Young, *The Shack*, 2005, Windblown Media, Newbury Park, CA 91320.

[7] **Words.** Rape, Abuse and Incest National Network, RAINN, 2008; www.rainn.org, accessed July 28, 2008.

[8] **Words.** www.prevent-abuse-now.com/stats/htm, accessed August 7, 2008.

[9] **Journey.** William Penn, *Fruits of Solitude, Part Two,* (§128-134), 1693, www.quakercenter.org/Pages/AboutUsPages/QuakersSpeak.htm, accessed May 10, 2009.

[10] **Edge.** www.cdc.gov/DES, accessed May 2, 2008.

[11] **Drummer.** "The Little Drummer Boy," words and music by Henry Onerati, Katherine Davis and Harry Simone, 1958. ©Copyright MCMLVIII, Mills Music, Inc., and Delaware Music Corp.

[12] **Arch.** www.visionsofjesuschrist.com/weeping286.htm, accessed June 8, 2008.

LaVergne, TN USA
13 November 2010
204661LV00003B/5/P